Englisch 9./10. Klasse

Martina Mattes

Die Zeiten – Bildung und Verwendung

Mit heraustrennbarem Lösungsteil

Mentor Übungsbuch 852

Mentor Verlag München

Die Autorin: Martina Mattes, Gymnasiallehrerin für Deutsch und Englisch, Dozentin für Literatur- und Medienpädagogik, Fachkoordinatorin für Englisch an bayerischen Fachakademien für Sozialpädagogik

Redaktion: Jana de Blank, Gabriele Jahn

Illustrationen: Henning Schöttke, Kiel

In neuer Rechtschreibung

Umwelthinweis: Gedruckt auf chlorfrei gebleichtem Papier

Layout: Peter Glaubitz, auf der Basis des Layouts von Barbara Slowik, München
Umschlag: Iris Steiner, München
Satz: OK Satz GmbH, Unterschleißheim
Druck: Landesverlag Druckservice, Linz

Auflage:	5.	4.	3.	2.	1.	Letzte Zahlen
Jahr:	2004	2003	2002	2001	2000	maßgeblich

© 2000 by Mentor Verlag Dr. Ramdohr KG, München
Printed in Germany • ISBN 3-580-63852-1

Inhaltsverzeichnis

Vorwort 5

1. Das Simple Present in Aussagesätzen 6
2. Das Simple Present in Fragesätzen und Verneinungen 8
3. Das Present Progressive 10
4. Die Unterscheidung zwischen Simple Present und Present Progressive 12
5. Das Passiv im Present Tense 14
6. Mixed exercises zum Present Tense 16
7. Das Simple Past 18
8. Das Past Progressive 20
9. Die Unterscheidung zwischen Simple Past und Past Progressive 22
10. Das Passiv im Past Tense 24
11. Mixed exercises zum Past Tense 26
12. Das Present Perfect Simple in Aussagesätzen 28
13. Das Present Perfect in Frage und Verneinung 30
14. Das Present Perfect Progressive 32
15. Das Passiv im Present Perfect 34
16. Die Unterscheidung zwischen Past Tense und Present Perfect 36
17. Past Tense oder Present Perfect? 38
18. Mixed exercises 40
19. Das Past Perfect 42
20. Die Unterscheidung zwischen Simple Past und Past Perfect 44
21. Die Formen von *to be* 46
22. Unregelmäßige Verben 48
23. Test zu den bisher gelernten Tenses 50
24. Übersicht über die Zeiten 52

Lösungsteil 55

Unser Tipp für alle, die noch mehr wissen wollen:

Mentor Lernhilfen

Die sind Spezialisten im Erklären und machen fit fürs ganze Schuljahr!

Für Englisch in der 9./10. Klasse gibt's die Bände:

The Final Touch 1 (9./10. Klasse)
Indirekte Rede, Gerundium, Infinitiv, Artikel, Adjektiv, Adverb
ISBN 3-580-63550-6

The Final Touch 2 (9./10. Klasse)
Relativsätze, Pluralformen, Hilfsverben, Partizip, Simple Past, Present Perfect,
Verlaufsform
ISBN 3-580-63551-4

Vorwort

Hallo, liebe Schülerin, lieber Schüler,

du möchtest dein Englisch ein bisschen trainieren, aber möglichst schnell und ohne viel Theorie? Dann bist du hier richtig – egal, ob du dich nun generell verbessern oder eines der Themen dieses Buches speziell für eine Klassenarbeit üben willst.

Du wirst sehen – jetzt geht's besonders easy:

Treffsicher — Dieses Buch ist in **24 kleine Lernportionen** gegliedert.
→ So findest du dich besonders schnell zurecht.

Übersichtlich — Jede Lernportion umfasst genau eine **Doppelseite**.
→ So hast du immer alles auf einen Blick.

Einleuchtend — Jede Doppelseite beginnt mit einer kurzen, klaren **Regel**.
→ So weißt du immer sofort, worauf es ankommt.

Clever — Dann geht's ans **Üben** – ganz locker, Schritt für Schritt.
→ So bereitest du dich optimal vor.

Praktisch — Der **Lösungsteil** zum Heraustrennen passt seitengetreu dazu.
→ So kontrollierst du blitzschnell – ohne Suchen und Blättern.

Am besten gleich loslegen!

Viel Spaß und ganz viel Erfolg

wünscht dir

dein Mentor Verlag

Noch ein Tipp — Du hast noch mehr Nachholbedarf, aber keine Lust auf Nachhilfe? Dann versuch's doch mit den **Mentor Lernhilfen**: Schau mal auf die Seite gegenüber!

1 Das Simple Present in Aussagesätzen

1. Die einfache Form des Simple Present – im Gegensatz zur Verlaufsform (Present Progressive, Kapitel 3) – zeigt an, dass jemand etwas **häufig**, **selten** oder **nie** tut.

   → Anna and Nicolas **play** tennis seven days a week.

2. Es beschreibt **allgemein gültige** Tatsachen und Wahrheiten.

   → The sun **rises** in the east.

3. Man verwendet es, um Handlungen zu schildern, die **nacheinander** geschehen.

   → First Mother **drives** the children to the train station, then they **take** a train to Wembley, and there all of them **watch** the tennis match.

Merke

Signalwörter sind: *never, rarely, seldom, occasionally, sometimes, often, frequently, every day/week/ month/year …, regularly, usually, normally, always* etc.

Übung 1

Bilde vollständige englische Sätze aus den angegebenen Satzteilen und verwende dabei das Simple Present.

1. Before / play golf / Nina and George / they / have lunch / at 12.30 / every day.
   Before they play golf Nina and George have lunch at 12.30 every day.

2. Nina's / handicap / be / 12 / George's / be / 13.

3. George / try to / take part in / golf tournaments / regularly.

4. Nina / sometimes / watch / Grand Prix racing / on TV.

5. She and her friend / like / car racing / but / they think / it / be / dangerous / very.

6. Ferrari and McLaren / be / very / in motor sport / successful teams.

6

Übung 2   Setze das richtige Verb in der richtigen Form ein.

fall – be – be interested in – can swim – can ride – work – be – cost – come to – have – pay

Canoeing and rock-climbing .... two of George's leisure activities. He often
.... into the water but he .... always .... to the bank (dt. Ufer). Nina
and many of her friends .... horseback-riding.
They .... several horses they .... 'Black Beauty' .... Nina's
favourite. It .... a lot of money to own a horse, so Nina .... in a fast
food restaurant every Saturday. With the money she .... the vet who
.... see 'Black Beauty' regularly.

Übung 3   Übersetze ins Englische.

1. Ich spiele gern Volleyball und ich bin sehr gut in diesem Sport.

....

2. Mein Bruder George und ich sind Mitglieder der Schulmannschaft.

....

3. Meine große Schwester Marla hasst alle Arten von Ballspielen.

....

4. Sie ist verrückt nach Pferden und schnellen Autos.

....

Übung 4   Übersetze ins Deutsche.

1. Hot-air balloons seem to fascinate everyone.

....

2. Ballooning is a wonderful but also an expensive hobby.

....

3. A new balloon can cost between $15,000 and $45,000.

....

4. After a safe landing the pilot and his passengers always drink a glass of champagne.

....

② Das Simple Present in Fragesätzen und Verneinungen

Frage und Verneinung von Vollverben werden im Simple Present so gebildet:

1. Frage: *do/does* + Subjekt + Grundform
2. Verneinung: Subjekt + *do* + *not* + Grundform

→ He knows the headmaster.
Does he know the headmaster?
He **doesn't know** (Kurzform von **does not know**) the headmaster.

Merke In der **gesprochenen Sprache** werden in der Regel **Kurzformen** verwendet wie *you don't, he hasn't, she's, they're* usw.

Übung 1 Bilde vollständige englische Sätze im Simple Present.

1. Most of the teachers / talk / too much?

....

2. The maths teacher / not give / homework / over the weekend.

....

3. He / not / believe / it / if / anyone / tell / him / that / maths / be / the most difficult subject in the world.

....

Übung 2 Setze das richtige Verb in der richtigen Form ein.

be – go to – not like – not like

Ralf: .... you .... a girls' school?

Mary: Oh, no, I don't. I go to a comprehensive school in the south of London.

Ralf: I heard that in England a lot of school children have to wear a school uniform but they .... it. Is that true?

Mary: I .... not so sure about that. My school uniform is pretty, but my brother .... his at all.

8

Übung 3   Forme die folgenden Fragen in verneinte Fragen um.

1. Does your homework take up most of your afternoon?

2. Do many of the pupils like German literature?

3. Why does the school provide us with free lunch?

Übung 4   Übersetze ins Englische.

1. Gehen viele französische Schulkinder auf Gesamtschulen?

2. Ich glaube nicht.

3. Kennen Sie ein berühmtes Internat?

4. Sind Winchester und Harrow Städte mit sehr teuren Schulen?

5. Besucht Prinz William eine Schule nahe dem Schloss seiner Großmutter?

Übung 5   Übersetze ins Deutsche.

1. I don't want to talk about the British school system.

2. Does your father really have to pay school fees for you?

3. Do their teachers have a lot of patience?

4. Laura does not have any difficulty with her English homework.

5. What do you think of Peter's attitude towards exams?

③ Das Present Progressive

Das Present Progressive drückt aus, dass etwas **zum gegenwärtigen Zeitpunkt** (also **gerade jetzt**) geschieht – im Gegensatz zu regelmäßig wiederkehrenden Vorgängen, die das Simple Present verlangen (vgl. auch Kap. 4).

→ What **is** Sarah **doing** at the moment? – She's **sending** a message.

Bildung

Subjekt	+	Form von *to be*	+	Grundform	+	ing
I		am		sending		a message.

Merke

Signalwörter sind: *look, now, at the moment, at present, just …*

Beachte: Im Deutschen gibt es keine Verlaufsform. Wir drücken mit Wörtern wie „im Augenblick, gerade, momentan …" aus, dass etwas gerade geschieht.

Übung 1

Du bist in einer Autofabrik in Detroit. Berichte in vollständigen Sätzen, was du gerade siehst.

1. Robots / put together / the parts of the cars.

2. Computers / control / the quality / of the work done on the assembly lines.

3. Engineers / check / the amount of time / needed by the workers.

Übung 2

Finde jeweils das richtige Verb. Setze die korrekte Form des Present Progressive ein.

try – improve – look forward to – just modernize – wait for

1. The Ford company .... its factory in Detroit.
2. Today the car industry .... to develop non-polluting cars.
3. New production lines .... the quality of the new cars.
4. Some factory workers .... the shift to start.
5. Other workers .... having a break.

Übung 3   Vervollständige dieses Telefongespräch.

Craig: Hi Wayne, I hope I .... (disturb) you at the moment.

Wayne: Well, I .... (try) to get some sleep. I was partying all night long.

Craig: And what .... (your Dad / do)?

Wayne: He .... (work) in his garage, I guess. He .... (probably / repair) his old Thunderbird. But why .... (call) so early in the morning?

Craig: I .... (desperately / try) to get some help. My Dad's Porsche .... (sit) at the bottom of our swimming pool and you or your Dad must help me.

Wayne: What? What .... (say)? You .... (joke), aren't you?

Craig: No, I'm not. I'm dead serious. I was a little drunk last night and I forgot to put on the handbrake and the Porsche slowly rolled down the drive into the swimming pool.

Wayne: Okay, okay, I'm on my way.

Übung 4   Verbinde die Sätze mit Hilfe des Present Progressive.

While the three men .... (pull) the Porsche out of the swimming pool, Craig's father comes back from his business trip. When he sees what .... (go on) he has a heart attack. Craig helps his father until the ambulance arrives. While they .... (hurry) to the hospital, Craig worries about what will happen. Fortunately, the driver .... (drive) fast so that they reach the hospital in time. While Craig's father .... (recover) from his shock, Craig and Wayne have the Porsche repaired. When Craig's father sees his Porsche again it .... (shine) like new.

4 Die Unterscheidung zwischen Simple Present und Present Progressive

Während das **Present Progressive** ausdrückt, was zu einem bestimmten Zeitpunkt in der Gegenwart gerade vor sich geht, drückt das **Simple Present** eine Handlung aus, die regelmäßig, oft oder nie passiert (vgl. Kap. 1, 2 und 3).

→ Mum: I'm afraid Cory is busy at the moment. She's **watching** her favorite series on TV. She **watches** it every Tuesday night.

Übung 1

Simple Present oder Present Progressive? Vervollständige die Unterhaltung zwischen Cory und Alison.

Cory: _____ (you / can / hear) those girls over there? _____ (they / talk) about us?

Alison: I _____ (not / think) so but maybe it _____ (be) a good idea to leave the party now. What _____ (you / think)?

Cory: I _____ (be / not sure). I usually really _____ (enjoy) parties but I _____ (enjoy) this one. The boys here _____ (be) a bit shy, and the other girls …

Alison: Why _____ (we / not / leave) and _____ (go to) my brother's party? He _____ (have) one right now in his beautiful apartment in Kensington.

Cory: I _____ (not / like) the idea.

Alison: Oh, come on. _____ (not / be) such a spoilsport (dt. Spielverderber)!

Cory: All right, then. But first I _____ (must / call) my parents. They always _____ (want / know) where I _____ (be). I _____ (wonder) what they _____ (do) at the moment. I hope they _____ (not / wait) for me.

Alison: Oh, you and your parents. Mine _____ (be) much less complicated. They _____ (not / care) what I _____ (be / do) as long as it _____ (not / be) illegal and I _____ (come) home every night.

Cory: Okay, let's go! But _____ (lend) me your mobile phone (dt. Handy) first, please.

Übung 2

Unterstreiche in Übung 1 die Signalwörter (siehe Kapitel 1, Seite 6 und Kapitel 3, Seite 10). **Schreibe sie auf.**

Signalwörter für das Simple Present in diesem Text:

....

Signalwörter für das Present Progressive in diesem Text:

....

Weitere Signalwörter für das Simple Present:

....

Weitere Signalwörter für das Present Progressive:

....

Übung 3

Wähle zwischen dem Simple Present und dem Present Progressive aus. Streiche die falsche Verbform durch.

1. Hey you! What are you staring at / do you stare at?
2. Why are you driving so fast / do you drive so fast? – Because we are late.
3. Can I turn the CD-player down? You are not listening / do not listen anyway.
4. What are you eating / do you eat? – I'm having a piece of cake.
5. Are you Swedish? – No, I'm coming / I come from Denmark.
6. How many languages do you speak / are you speaking?
7. When does school usually start / is school usually starting in Denmark?
8. What are you doing / do you do right now? – Are you blind? I am playing cards / I play cards with Joe.

Übung 4

Noch ein Dialog zwischen Cory und Alison auf der Party von Alisons Bruder. Benutze das Simple Present oder das Present Progressive.

Alison: Oh, I .... (love) this party. The people here are so cool.

Cory: Look! .... (not / be) that Elton John over there?

Alison: Listen! He .... (sing) his latest song with the Spice Girls. And look over there! Mick Jagger .... (kiss) a blonde lady.

Cory: Wow, and what .... (your brother / do)? He .... (hold) hands with Tina Turner.

Alison: If I .... (not / see) this with my own eyes, I wouldn't believe it.

5 Das Passiv im Present Tense

Während das Aktiv eine Tätigkeit ausdrückt, die das Subjekt ausführt, bezeichnet das Passiv eine Tätigkeit, die am Subjekt vollzogen wird. Dem deutschen „von" bzw. „durch" entspricht das englische **by**.

Bildung

Das Passiv wird wie folgt gebildet:
Subjekt   **Form von** *to be* + **Past Participle** + (*by*)

These tankers   **are**   **built**   *by a famous engineering company.*

Entsprechend lautet die Verlaufsform:
This tanker   **is being**   **built**   *in Hamburg.*

Übung 1   Gib das Past Participle an.

find, found, ...   drill, drilled, ...

join, joined, ...   drink, drank, ...

catch, caught, ...   build, built, ...

be, was/were, ...

Übung 2   Finde Antworten zu diesen Fragen. Benutze die vorgegebenen Wörter und das Passiv der Verben in Klammern.

1. What can happen when an oil tanker loses tons of oil in the open sea?
   (A lot of / birds and animals / kill)

2. Who lays the pipelines in the North Sea?
   (Men / on special ships / hire / for that)

3. Do they need tankers for the transportation?
   (Yes / tankers / use / to bring / oil / on shore)

4. How is energy often wasted in your home?
   (Radios / often / not switch off / and lights / leave on)

14

Übung 3

Vervollständige die folgenden Sätze, indem du die angegebenen Verben im Passiv benutzt.

leuve – need   pay – toss around

1. Lots of workers _____ for the work on the platforms.

2. High wages _____ by the oil companies.

3. The platform cannot _____ by the workers unless they have permission from their boss.

4. In bad weather or in a heavy storm the men working on the platform

_____ .

Übung 4

Heinz und John unterhalten sich über ihre Arbeit auf einer Bohrinsel. Kannst du dolmetschen?

John: I'm forced to stay in this unfriendly place for at least two more months.

_____

Heinz: Das ist wirklich schlimm.

_____

John: I'm employed as a diver, and I'm the only one on board here who can dive.

_____

_____

Heinz: Aber kannst du nicht einfach abhauen?

_____

John: No, that's impossible. But my days here are counted, believe me.

_____

Übung 5

Wie sagst du auf Englisch,

1. … dass das Rauchen auf einer Ölbohrinsel nicht erlaubt ist?

_____

2. … dass du wissen möchtest, wie Benzin aus Rohöl gewonnen wird?

_____

3. … dass heutzutage immer noch neue Ölfelder gefunden werden können?

_____

4. … dass auf Ölbohrinseln kein Alkohol getrunken werden darf?

_____

6 Mixed Exercises zum Present Tense

Übung 1 Vervollständige die Sätze. Verwende das Simple Present oder das Present Progressive der Verben in Klammern.

John Taylor .... (be) an English engineer. He .... (specialize) in drilling for oil in the North Sea. This year he .... (work) on an oil rig, which .... (call) 'Blet Sar'. He .... (do not / speak) any Norwegian, but he .... (try) to learn at least some of the most important words. John .... (know) that he .... (earn) good money but he .... (miss) his wife and four children very much. He usually .... (like) his work, but at the moment it .... (rain) heavily and no work .... (can / do) on the oil rig. Right now John and his Norwegian friends .... (play) Monopoly so that they .... (not feel) lonely.

Übung 2 John Taylor bekommt einen Brief von seiner kleinen Tochter. Setze die Verben ins Simple Present oder ins Present Progressive.

Dear Daddy,

I .... (miss) you so much. Life .... (be) boring without you. .... (like) your job in the North Sea? I .... (hate) it because it .... (take) you away from me. While I .... (write) this, I .... (cry) the whole time. I .... (feel) so lonely at the moment. Sorry that the letter .... (have) so many watery spots. These .... (be) my tears.

Please, Daddy, come back soon!

Lots of love, Priscilla

P.S. Mummy .... (want) me to say hello to you for her.

Übung 3

Vervollständige die folgenden Sätze durch die aktive oder passive Form der Verben in Klammern.

1. Sometimes children ………………………………… (talk to) as if they are stupid.
2. Do you think these kids ………… (be) capable of doing it all by themselves?
3. The young people of today ……………………………… (feel not) miserable because they believe they will have a wonderful future.
4. Boys and girls ………… (have) equal educational opportunities, as ……………………………… (require) by law.
5. It ………… (be not) reasonable for girls ……………………………… (refuse) entry into an all-male club.

Übung 4

Übersetze die fehlenden Satzteile.

1. ……………………………………………………………………… (Viele Schüler an deutschen Gymnasien denken) that speaking English as the English do ……………………………… (ist schwierig).
2. ……………………………………………………………………… (Es gibt eine Menge Wörter) the pupils have never heard of.
3. ……………………………………………………………………… (Während der Schulaufgabe [test] wünschen sich die meisten Schüler) that they had studied more.
4. ……………………………………………………………………… (Es ist allgemein bekannt) that English is one of the easiest languages in the world.
5. ……………………………… (Weißt du) how many people in the world speak English?
6. In almost every continent ……………………………… (gibt es mindestens eine Nation) whose mother tongue is English.
7. ……………………………………………………………………… (Englisch wird auf der ganzen Welt gesprochen).
8. ……………………………………………………………………… (Magst du die englische Sprache)?

7 Das Simple Past

Das Simple Past bezeichnet Vorgänge oder Handlungen, die der Vergangenheit angehören und in ihr völlig abgeschlossen wurden. Es wird auch verwendet, wenn man wiederholte Handlungen oder eine Reihenfolge von Ereignissen oder Handlungen beschreiben will.

→ Yesterday evening I **prepared** myself to go out. I **put** on my new shirt and trousers. And then Kevin **called** to say that he couldn't pick me up.

Merke

Signalwörter sind: *yesterday, ago, last week/month/year, the other day* (dt. neulich), *in 1984, when I was a little girl* etc.

Übung 1   Setze die Sätze in das Simple Past.

1. The lady gets up at six o'clock in the morning.

2. She has a shower and has breakfast.

3. She drinks tea and eats toast with butter.

4. Every morning a friend stops in front of her house and takes her to work.

Übung 2   Deine Freundin kommt aus Amerika zurück, wo sie als Aupairmädchen gearbeitet hat. Stelle ihr Fragen über ihren Aufenthalt.

1. How long / you / stay / in the United States?

2. Like / it / you / there?

3. How many / new friends / you / make?

Übung 3

Welches Wort passt am besten? Setze die korrekte Form im Simple Past ein.

be – offer – pay – get – go   spend – buy – accept – be unemployed

Last month I .... to the unemployment office. They .... me a job

and I .... it at once. I .... for several

months but now I am working as a waitress. Last week I .... my first pay cheque.

Yesterday I .... it all on beautiful clothes. I .... a blue dress, a green

T-shirt and a really great skirt. I .... $45. Yesterday .... a wonderful day.

Übung 4

Erzähle die folgende Geschichte auf Englisch.

1. 1998 arbeitete ich ein Jahr lang als Aupairmädchen in New York.

....

2. Mir hat es dort nicht gefallen.

....

3. Die Familie, bei der ich arbeitete, wohnte in einer sehr lauten Straße in Manhattan.

....

....

4. Ich war froh, als das Jahr vorbei war.

....

Übung 5

Stelle nun folgende Fragen zu der Geschichte in Englisch.

1. Wo hast du 1998 gearbeitet?

....

2. Hat es dir in New York gefallen?

....

3. Wie war das Wetter?

....

4. Wie bist du mit der Familie zurechtgekommen?

....

8 Das Past Progressive

Das Past Progressive drückt aus, was zu einem bestimmten Zeitpunkt in der Vergangenheit gerade vor sich ging. Oft verwendet man das Past Progressive für eine Hintergrundhandlung, die bereits ablief, als ein neues Ereignis eintrat (Simple Past).

→ Inspector: What **were** you **doing** at 11 p.m. last Sunday?
Diana: I **was sitting** on the sofa in my living room and **listening** to the radio, when I heard the sound of breaking glass.

Bildung

Subjekt	was/were	+ Grundform	+ ing
The earth	was	shaking.	

Übung 1

Hier ist aufgelistet, wie Diana gestern ihren Morgen verbrachte. Bilde Sätze, die angeben, was sie zu den bestimmten Zeiten gerade getan hat.

6.00–6.08 took a shower
6.15–6.18 got dressed
6.35–6.39 ran to the train station
6.40–7.35 sat in the train

1. At 6.03 o'clock ....

2. At 6.16 o'clock ....

3. At 6.37 o'clock ....

4. At 7 o'clock ....

Übung 2

Schreibe auf, was Diana gestern gerade machte (Past Progressive), als etwas anderes plötzlich passierte (Simple Past).

1. Diana / stand / in the shower / when / go out / the lights.

....

2. She / put on / her new blouse / when / come off / a button.

....

3. have breakfast / Diana / when / the telephone / ring.

....

4. She / the house / leave / when / she / a shout / hear.

....

Übung 3   Sylvia und ein paar Leute befanden sich gerade in einem Hotel in San Francisco, als die Erde bebte. Bilde mit den angegebenen Wörtern Sätze, in denen du angibst, was gleichzeitig passierte.

1. Sylvia / on the phone / talk / while / the earth / shake.

....

2. Sylvia's father / stare out of the hotel window / as the Bay Bridge / collapse.

....

3. Two men / try / steal / expensive diamonds / while / the owner / in the hotel restaurant / have dinner.

....

....

Übung 4   Sylvia schildert ihrer amerikanischen Freundin Diana, was während des Erdbebens in San Francisco alles passierte. Kannst du dolmetschen?

Sylvia: Der Fußboden zitterte und wir merkten, dass es ein Erdbeben war.

....

Diana: What were you doing at the time?

....

....

Sylvia: Mein Bruder und meine Schwester spielten gerade Schach, meine Mutter schrieb an ihrem Roman und ich badete den Hund.

....

....

Diana: It sounds incredible. Were you really bathing the dog while an earthquake was going on?

....

....

Sylvia: Ja. Aber der Hund spielte verrückt. Nach dem Beben versteckte er sich die ganze Nacht lang unter meinem Bett.

....

....

9   Die Unterscheidung zwischen Simple Past und Past Progressive

Das Past Progressive und das Simple Past werden oft zusammen in einem Satz verwendet, wenn ausgedrückt werden soll, dass eine Handlung zu einem vergangenen Zeitpunkt **gerade vor sich ging** (Past Progressive), als eine andere Handlung (im **Simple Past**) **plötzlich** einsetzte.

→ We **were having** dinner when the lights **went** out.

Übung 1

Bilde Sätze aus den angegebenen Wörtern. Setze die Verben in die richtige Form des Past Tense.

1. What / you / do / this time yesterday?

2. I / pack / my suitcase / for our trip to Wales, / and ...

3. ... my sister Friederike / the Internet / surf / for info about Cardiff.

4. She / anything / find?

5. No / not. / She / just / chat / with a Welshman / when / her computer crash.

Übung 2

Setze das richtige Verb in der richtigen Zeit ein.

climb – head for – hurt – want to – keep falling – travel

While we .... Wales, my brother .... to Scotland. He .... climb Ben Nevis, the highest mountain in Scotland. But while he .... Ben Nevis some rocks .... down. Fortunately, nobody ....

Übung 3

Helen unterhält sich mit ihrer Freundin Sue über ihre Ferien in Wales. Setze die richtigen Verbformen des Past Tense ein.

Helen: .... (you / have) a nice holiday?

Sue: Oh, yes. It .... (be) great.

Helen: Where .... (you / be) exactly?

Sue: First we .... (go) by plane to London, then we .... (rent) a car
and .... (drive) to Cymru the same day.

Helen: What .... (you / say)?

Sue: We .... (travel) to Wales, which is called Cymru in Welsh. We
.... (stay) in a haunted castle with lots of ghosts. When they
.... (rattle) their chains, nobody ....
.... (can / sleep). Old Faithful, one of the ghosts, ...
.... (just / follow) me, when he .... (drop)
his head. Another one .... (come after) my
little sister when he .... (fall) over a big wooden chest.

Helen: .... (be / not / you) afraid?

Sue: No, I .... (be / not). I .... (have) a lot of fun.

Übung 4

Übersetze folgende Sätze. Beachte den Unterschied zwischen dem Simple Past und dem Past Progressive.

1. Als es zwölf Uhr schlug, lagen wir schon in unsere Betten.

....

2. Suddenly the door opened.

....

3. Ein Geist mit seinem Kopf unter seinem Arm kam langsam herein.

....

4. I turned on the lights and the creature disappeared for ever.

....

5. In der nächsten Nacht konnten wir ruhig und ungestört schlafen.

....

10 Das Passiv im Past Tense

1. Das Passiv im Simple Past wird verwendet, um zu sagen, dass eine Handlung in der Vergangenheit **oft** oder **immer wieder** ausgeführt wurde.
   → Hurricane "George" hit Miami last night. A bridge was damaged and several trees were uprooted.

2. Das Past Progressive im Passiv beschreibt eine Handlung, die sich **in einem bestimmten Zeitraum** in der Vergangenheit abspielte. Sie ist **abgeschlossen** und hat keinen Bezug zur Gegenwart mehr.
   → Warnings were being given out by the police all night.

Bildung

1. Passiv im Simple Past:
   Subjekt + was/were + Past Participle
   A bridge   was   damaged.

2. Passiv des Past Progressive
   Subjekt + was/were + being + Past Participle
   Warnings   were   being   given out.

Übung 1

„Fliegender Pfeil", ein alter Sioux-Indianer, erzählt von seiner Kindheit. Setze die richtigen Verbformen ein.

When I was seven years old, I _____ (allow) to go to school for the first time in my life. My brothers and I went to a building that _____ (build) by white settlers. At the door we _____ (welcome) by a nice young woman who _____ (call) "Madame" by the other schoolchildren. I was very excited and I liked school a lot. One day, as our maths tests _____ (just / return), there was a terrible noise outside. After a while the sound _____ (can / not / hear) any more. Then there it was again. Suddenly the door _____ (open) wide by a big grizzly. Another big roar (dt. Gebrüll) _____ (hear), and then there was a shot. Our teacher was standing there with a gun in her hands. The animal _____ (shoot) by our brave schoolteacher. We _____ each _____ (allow) to take a tooth from the bear. I will remember this incident and this woman all my life.

Übung 2
Simple Past oder Past Progressive? Übersetze die folgenden Fragen zu der Geschichte aus Übung 1.

1. Wann wurde „Fliegender Pfeil" in die Schule geschickt?

2. Von wem wurde die Schule gebaut?

3. Wer (!) hat ihn unterrichtet?

4. Wie wurde seine Lehrerin genannt?

5. Von welchem Tier wurde der Unterricht eines Tages gestört?

6. Welche Schulaufgaben wurden gerade zurückgegeben, als der Bär hereinkam?

7. Wer erschoss den Grizzlybären? (Passiv!)

8. Wer durfte die Zähne behalten? (Übersetze: Wem wurde es erlaubt, …)

9. Wann wurde dieses Abenteuer erzählt?

10. Von wem wurde die Geschichte erzählt?

Übung 3
Übersetze ins Englische.

1. Mir und meinen Geschwistern wurden viele alte Geschichten erzählt.

2. Eine wurde von uns allen besonders geliebt.

3. Es war die Geschichte von dem Indianer „Adlerauge", der von einem Wolf aufgezogen und ernährt wurde.

11 Mixed Exercises zum Past Tense

Übung 1   Setze die richtige Verbform in der richtigen Zeit ein.

fascinate – be born – call – develop – found – leave – announce – buy

1. Bill Gates .... in Seattle, Washington, in the year 1955.

2. At the age of 12 he .... already .... by computers.

3. In 1975 Bill Gates and his partner Paul Allen .... a computer-

   programming language .... BASIC.

4. In the same year Bill Gates .... Harvard University to have more time for his
   company, Microsoft.

5. In 1989 the Corbis Corporation .... by Gates.

6. Six years later this company .... 16 million photographic images and plans

   .... to digitize a lot of them.

Übung 2   Übersetze die fehlenden Satzteile.

1. (Gestern schrieb Tom gerade auf seinem Computer) ....

   .... when it suddenly
   crashed.

2. (Er rief seine Freundin Celine an, die versprach) ....

   .... to come to his house
   immediately.

3. After a couple of minutes ....
   (wurde der Fehler von Celine gefunden).

4. They were playing on the computer ....

   .... (als ein lauter Schrei zu hören war).

5. Tom's mother ....

   .... (hatte ebenfalls gerade mit ihrem Computer Schwierigkeiten).

6. (Auch Toms Mutter konnte von Celine geholfen werden) ....

   ....

Übung 3

Zwei Schüler, Celine und Tom, unterhalten sich über die gestrige Prüfung. Setze die richtigen Verbformen ein.

Celine: Hi, Tom. How .... (it / go) in yesterday's exam?

Tom: Well, in the beginning I .... (think) that I .... (have) all the right answers, but then I .... (see) what the others had written and now I know that I might have failed (*to fail an exam:* eine Prüfung nicht bestehen).

Celine: .... (you / revise) enough?

Tom: Oh yes, I think so. My mother .... (help / me) a lot and even my Dad .... (study) with me. He .... (listen) for over two hours to what I .... (tell) him about the Boston Tea Party and its consequences. But what about you?

Celine: I think I .... (do) alright. In the exam I .... (ask) about Thanksgiving and I .... (be able to tell) the teachers a lot. They .... (be quite pleased) with me.

Tom: You lucky girl. Why .... (I / not / ask) by my teachers about easy stuff like Thanksgiving? I would have known almost everything about that, but in my exam I .... (can / remember / almost) nothing about a war that .... (take place) more than 200 years ago.

Celine: If I were you, I wouldn't worry too much. I'm sure you will pass the exam. By the way, ... (do) you and your friends .... (celebrate) the end of the schoolyear yesterday?

Tom: Yes, we .... (do). We .... (party) all night long. Why .... (be / not / you) there?

Celine: I .... (be / not) there because I .... (not / invite).

Tom: Oh, Celine! I'm so sorry.

12 Das Present Perfect Simple in Aussagesätzen

Das Present Perfect Simple wird verwendet, um anzuzeigen, dass eine Handlung, die in der Vergangenheit begann, in irgendeiner Form einen **Bezug zur Gegenwart** hat.

→ Karen **has been** to Boston three times so far.

Bildung

Subjekt +	have/has	+ Past Participle	
We	**have** never	**been**	to Boston before.

Merke

Signalwörter sind unbestimmte Zeitangaben, die sowohl die Vergangenheit als auch die Gegenwart umfassen, wie z. B.: *just now, lately, recently, already, finally, at last, this morning* (alle Verbindungen mit *this* und *these* + Zeitangaben), *today, ever, never, always, so far, yet, since* und *for*. Im Deutschen wird das Present Perfect oft auch mit dem Präsens übersetzt.

Übung 1   Bilde vollständige englische Sätze im Present Perfect.

1. Aunt Margie / try to call / us / from Boston / several times / today.

....

2. She / not see / us / since 1985.

....

Übung 2   Finde jeweils das richtige Verb. Setze die richtige Form im Present Perfect ein.

live – know – be terrible – never have – invite – accept – never visit

1. We .... guests from America before.
2. We .... Aunt Margie several times.
3. But this is the first time she .... our invitation.
4. Aunt Margie .... on the East Coast all her life.
5. She .... Germany before.
6. The weather in Boston .... for over a week now.
7. Aunt Margie .... us since we were babies.

Übung 3   Übersetze ins Englische und verwende das Present Perfect.

1. Die Kinder haben ihre Tante endlich wieder gesehen.

2. Sie hat ihnen ein Buch über Boston mitgebracht.

3. Margie ist bis jetzt dreizehn Mal in Europa gewesen.

4. Sie hat schon viele Städte und Länder gesehen.

5. Sie spielt jetzt seit 20 Jahren Geige bei den Bostoner Philharmonikern.

6. Ihr Bruder dirigiert seit 1989 die Boston Pops.

7. Wir haben versucht, Karten für das Festival zu bekommen, aber es ist uns noch nicht gelungen.

Übung 4   Übersetze ins Deutsche.

1. I have read the biography of John F. Kennedy, who was born in Boston.

2. Up to now we have never been to Canada, but we have been to almost every state in the US.

3. Sarah has been a tourist guide in Boston for five months now.

4. Have you ever followed the Freedom Trail in Boston city center?

13 Das Present Perfect in Frage und Verneinung

Auch Fragen und verneinte Sätze im Present Perfect schlagen eine Brücke zwischen Vergangenheit und Gegenwart.

→ **Have** you ever **skied** in Austria? – No, I **have never done** that.

Bildung

Frage:	**have/has** + Subjekt + Past Participle
Verneinung:	Subjekt + **have/has not** + Past Participle

Übung 1

Since oder *for*? – Erinnere dich: *since* bezeichnet einen Zeitpunkt, *for* eine Zeitspanne bzw. einen Zeitraum.

Suzi has not been in Salzburg .... six months. Her boyfriend has been a skiing instructor .... he was 19 years old. Because there are so many people who want to take skiing lessons, she has not seen him .... November, but today is his day off and he and Suzi have been skiing .... at least four hours. Now they are very tired. They go back to the hotel-room where Suzi has been staying .... more than a week now. She turns on her lap-top and goes online, but nobody has mailed her .... yesterday. Suddenly his mobile phone *(dt. Handy)* rings and somebody says that there has been a terrible accident in the mountains. Four people have been buried under masses of snow .... a quarter of an hour. This is the worst accident .... 1998 when two teenagers were missing .... more than three days.

Übung 2

Dein Freund ist Skilehrer in Österreich. Bilde aus den angegebenen Wörtern Fragen im Present Perfect.

1. How many times / be / you / to Austria before?

....

2. One of your students / an accident / have / ever?

....

3. How long / you / a skiing instructor / be?

....

4. You / a lot of money / earn / so far?

....

Übung 3

Im Werbeprospekt eines Skiortes in den Alpen kommen die folgenden Sätze vor. Übersetze sie für einen englischen Freund, der dorthin reisen möchte.

1. Haben Sie schon einmal daran gedacht, Ihren Urlaub in unserem hübschen Ort zu verbringen?

2. Wir wetten, dass Sie noch nie einen schöneren Sonnenuntergang in den Bergen gesehen haben!

3. Und warum haben Sie noch nicht unsere weltberühmten Knödel *(engl. dumpling)* probiert?

4. Unsere Gäste haben sich noch nie über lange Schlangen an den Skiliften beschwert!

5. Und hohe Preise haben sie hier auch noch nicht bezahlt!

Übung 4

Setze die richtigen Verbformen und *since* oder *for* in dieses Gespräch zwischen Nancy und Lawrence ein.

N: Joe went skiing two days ago. _____ you _____ (hear) from him so far?

L: No, I _____ (not / see) him _____ last Friday.

N: He wanted to call me, but he _____ (not / do) so yet.

L: Don't worry too much. I _____ (know) Joe _____ ages and

he _____ (never / keep) his promises.

N: I heard on the news this morning that the weather _____

(change) in the place where he has been staying _____ two days now.

L: All right then. I have the number of his mobile phone. Let's call him.

Das Present Perfect Progressive

 Das Present Perfect Progressive wird verwendet, um über die **Dauer** von Handlungen oder Vorgängen zu sprechen, die in der Vergangenheit angefangen haben und einen **Bezug zur Gegenwart** aufweisen.

→ I **have been sending** e-mails all morning.

Bildung

Subjekt + **have/has been** + Grundform + *ing*

Merke

In der deutschen Übersetzung benutzt man meist das Präsens zusammen mit dem Wort „schon".

Übung 1

Die königliche Hochzeit wird gerade im Fernsehen übertragen. Welcher der deutschen Sätze ist richtig? Kreuze an.

1. I have been watching the Royal Wedding for two hours now.
   ○ Ich schaue die königliche Hochzeit seit zwei Stunden an.
   ○ Ich schaue die königliche Hochzeit jetzt schon seit zwei Stunden an.
   ○ Ich schaute die königliche Hochzeit zwei Stunden an.

2. The sun has been shining since the wedding began.
   ○ Die Sonne scheint schon seit dem Beginn der Hochzeit.
   ○ Die Sonne schien seit dem Beginn der Hochzeit.
   ○ Die Sonne schien gerade, als die Hochzeit begann.

3. The prince has been staring at his bride ever since she entered the church.
   ○ Der Prinz starrt seine Braut an, seitdem sie die Kirche betrat.
   ○ Der Prinz starrte seine Braut seit ihrem Betreten der Kirche an.
   ○ Der Prinz hat seine Braut angestarrt, als sie die Kirche betrat.

4. The Queen Mother has been crying since the couple exchanged rings.
   ○ Die Königinmutter weinte, seit das Paar die Ringe getauscht hat.
   ○ Die Königinmutter weint, seitdem das Paar die Ringe tauschte.
   ○ Die Königinmutter hat geweint, als das Paar die Ringe getauscht hat.

Übung 2

Present Perfect Simple oder Present Perfect Progressive?
Setze die richtige Form ein.

Ute: Hey, Tony, you look tired. ....

(you / work) hard the last few days?

Tony: Oh no. Quite the opposite. I .... (just / arrive)

from Los Angeles. It was wonderful over there. I was visiting my big sister. She is a

famous actress. She .... (appear) in several films.

Ute: Wow, I'm impressed. It .... (be / always) my

dream to go there and become a star. How often ....

(you / be) to L.A.?

Tony: I .... (be) there twice. I ....

(come back) this morning. By the way, I ....

(have read) the book you gave me months ago, but I ....

.... (finish) it yet.

Ute: You can keep it. But let's talk about your sister. How long ....

.... (live) in California?

Tony: Suzanne – that's my sister's name – .... (live) in

Beverly Hills for more than five years now. Her husband founded a big studio and

he .... (successfully / head)

it for a long time now. When I was visiting them he even offered me a small part in

the latest movie with Julia Roberts.

Ute: This is hard to believe.

Tony: No, seriously. I .... (take) dance lessons since

I was five. For 15 years now I .... (dance)

every Friday and Saturday. I am a very good dancer. I .... just ....

(win) the national championships for the third time. Don't you believe me?

Ute: Oh, come on. ....

(you / really / dance) for such a long time?

Tony: Yeah, sure. Let's dance, and I'll show you!

33

15 Das Passiv im Present Perfect

Das Passiv im Present Perfect beschreibt, was mit einer Person bzw. Sache in der Vergangenheit **geschehen ist**.
Dieses Geschehen hat bis in die Gegenwart noch seine Bedeutung.

→ This film **has been produced by** a man called Broccoli.

Bildung

Subjekt + *have/has been* + Past Participle

Übung 1   Bilde vollständige englische Sätze im Present Perfect Passive.

1. Up to now / Universal Studios / visit / millions of people.

2. More science fiction movies / than love stories / in recent years / show.

3. How many films / direct / Steven Spielberg / so far?

4. Why / Tom Cruise / not award / yet / an Oscar?

5. So far / the latest James Bond movie / see / over 2,000,000 people.

6. Hundreds of thousands of young actors / attract / over the years / Hollywood.

Übung 2   Setze das richtige Verb im Present Perfect Passive ein.

rent – talk about – just open – invite – fire – hire – sell – exchange

1. A new cinema .... in Hatfield.
2. The new film .... for weeks now.
3. The actress Meg Ryan .... and Julia Roberts
   .... instead. Since then not a word
   .... between the two ladies.
4. .... the rights to the film .... to other countries yet?
5. At least 100 cars .... so far during the filming of the new James Bond movie.
6. .... you ever .... to a film premiere?

Übung 3   Finde die Fehler, streiche sie an und verbessere die Sätze.

1. She has never be seen in a cowboy film before.

   ....

2. These horses have not been yet trained.

   ....

3. Hugh Grant's last film have been in production for over nine months now.

   ....

4. It has been directed of a very famous woman.

   ....

Übung 4   Übersetze folgende Sätze.

1. Spielbergs neuester Film ist als „exzellent" bezeichnet worden.

   ....

2. Dieser Film ist für sechs Oscars nominiert worden.

   ....

35

16 Die Unterscheidung zwischen Past Tense und Present Perfect

Das **Past Tense** drückt aus, was zu einem bestimmten Zeitpunkt in der Vergangenheit geschehen und jetzt **vorbei** ist.
Das **Present Perfect** beschreibt dagegen, dass etwas in der Vergangenheit geschehen ist, das noch in irgendeiner Form einen **Bezug zur Gegenwart** hat.

→ Two months ago I   **met**   my boy-friend for the first time.

→ Since then we   **have seen**   each other every day.

Übung 1   Verbinde die zueinander passenden Sätze mit einer Linie.

Robin Hood was once   was called Little John.
He and his men   to hunt and fish in Sherwood Forest.
His best friend   seen Kevin Costner as Robin Hood?
The outlaws never   was married to Robin Hood.
His men wore green   lived of the rich people who passed by.
They never kept   robbed or hurt the poor and needy.
Maid Marian   the stolen things for themselves.
Robin and his men liked   a rich man, but he lost all his money.
Have you ever   so that it was difficult to see them in the forest.

Übung 2   Bilde vollständige Sätze und verwende die richtigen Vergangenheitsformen.

1. Ever / you / hear / of Robin Hood?

   ....

2. He / be / a brave and noble man / who / fight for the poor.

   ....

3. In Sherwood Forest / there / be / a camp / where all the outlaws / live / at that time.

   ....

4. Robin / love / by everyone?

   ....

5. Why / steal / Robin Hood / money / from the rich?

   ....

36

Übung 3   Streiche die falsche Form durch und verbessere die Sätze.

1. I did not see a film about Robin Hood in years.

....

2. Robin Hood's life was filmed about 20 times so far.

....

3. Friar Tuck and Little John have always accompanied Robin.

....

4. The merry man of Nottingham has loved his wife madly.

....

5. In the 14th century Edward II has been King of England.

....

6. Have you seen Robin Hood's statue in Nottingham?

....

Übung 4   Setze die richtige Verbform ein.

One day when Robin Hood .... (ride) with Little John through

Sherwood Forest they .... (hear) loud voices. They .... (come) closer and

.... (see) two ladies on white horses. The women ....

(surround) by three soldiers who .... (have) swords in their hands. "Go away!" one

of the ladies .... (shout). "We .... (be) on our horses

for more than two hours and we ....

(not want / return) to where we .... (come) from. Let us pass!" But the soldiers

.... (not allow) them to continue their ride through the

forest. Robin and Little John .... (fight) with the soldiers, ...

(defeat) them and .... (rescue) the two ladies. These two women

.... (give) Robin a golden ring as a gift because they .... (be)

so grateful. In those days a lot of people .... (worship)

Robin Hood and .... (think) he .... (be) a great hero.

17 Past Tense oder Present Perfect?

Übung 1 Setze in diesem Dialog zwischen Frank und Karen die richtige Zeit ein.

Frank: Hi, Karen! We .... (not / see) each other for a long time.

Karen: Yes, you're right. The last time we .... (meet) .... (be) at my sister's birthday party last September.

Frank: That's right. I even remember the topic we .... (talk about).

Karen: What .... (be) it? I can't remember.

Frank: Robin Hood and his life in the Middle Ages.

Karen: When .... (you / hear) about him for the first time?

Frank: I .... (hear) about Robin Hood in kindergarten. Our teacher .... (teach) us a song about Robin and Maid Marian and since then I .... (read) a lot about him.

Karen: .... (you / know) that his father .... (be) a brave knight?

Frank: Is that true?

Karen: About 100 years ago people .... (not / know) exactly where his place of birth .... (be) but then they .... (find) his grave in Nottingham.

Frank: No, that's not true. I .... (read) in the newspaper only last week that his grave .... (not / find) yet, and that they are still looking for it.

Karen: Do you know whether the Sheriff of Nottingham ever .... (catch) Robin?

Frank: Yes, I do. I .... (hear) in the news only a couple of days ago that the Sheriff .... (can never get hold of) Robin.

38

Übung 2   Vervollständige das Telefongespräch zwischen Mark und Sue.

Mark: Hello, Sue. This is Mark. _____ (you / finish) your homework yet?

Sue: Yes, I _____ (have). It _____ (be) very difficult to write a dialogue between Robin Hood and the Sheriff of Nottingham. At first I _____ (not / know) what I should write about them, but then my little brother _____ (come) into my room and _____ (disturb) me and suddenly I _____ (know) what the two _____ (say) to each other.

Mark: You're lucky. Yesterday I _____ (be) in the public library and I _____ (find) a very interesting book there on the Romans and the Saxons. Unfortunately it _____ (not / say) a single word about Robin Hood. Now I _____ (think) about this stupid dialogue for hours and my mind is a blank.

Sue: Don't give up, Mark. I'll help you.

Mark: That's very kind of you. I _____ (already / write) the beginning of the conversation. Listen, please, and tell me whether you like it or not. "On October 14th, 1066, Duke William of Normandy _____ (meet) and _____ (defeat) the English army at Hastings, where he _____ (kill) King Harold. On Christmas Day a bishop _____ (crown) him in Westminster Abbey. From then on his new name _____ (be) William I. Later he _____ (become know) as William the Conqueror."

Sue: That's very interesting but you _____ (not / mention) one single word about Robin so far, have you?

Mark: Oh Sue, you're very impatient. I _____ (tell) you just a couple of minutes ago that this dialogue is terribly hard for me.

Sue: Well, why don't you come to my house and we'll do your homework together?

Mark: That sounds wonderful. Thank you so much. I'll be over in a sec.

18   Mixed Exercises

Übung 1   Setze das richtige Verb in der richtigen Zeit ein.

be – have – used to – call – be – play – sing – write – be – give – win – be – play

When Tom .... a bit younger, he .... do a lot of sports, but now he

.... no time for that because every other night he .... in a band in his home-

town of Liverpool. The band .... the "Easy Beets". Besides Tom there

.... William, the guitarist, James, who .... the piano, and Tom's girlfriend

Fiona, who .... and .... beautiful songs about life and love. The

three .... so successful that last year they even .... a music contest. The best

music group .... a gold medal by Paul McCartney, who .... one of

the most famous pop stars in the world.

Übung 2   Übersetze ins Englische.

1. Liverpool hat schon immer jungen Musikern die Chance gegeben, vor einem Publikum
   zu spielen.

   ....

   ....

2. Vor acht Jahren fand der erste Musikwettbewerb für talentierte Jugendliche statt.

   ....

   ....

3. Es gibt einige Gruppen, deren Karriere vor Jahren in einem Pub begonnen hat.

   ....

   ....

4. Natürlich wollen alle jungen Musiker Plattenverträge bekommen.

   ....

   ....

5. Aber die meisten von ihnen machen Musik, weil es ihnen einfach großen Spaß macht.

   ....

   ....

Übung 3

Vervollständige den Dialog zwischen Fiona und ihrer Mutter. Benutze dabei die Wörter in Klammern.

Fiona: Mum, I'm going to wash the dishes now.

Mum: That's okay, Fiona. I _____ (do / already) it. Are you going to see Grandpa tonight?

Fiona: No, I _____ (see) him yesterday.

Mum: Fiona, _____ (read / yet) today's newspaper _____?

Fiona: Yes, I _____ (have) and it _____ (seem) as if I _____ (find) an apartment for Tom and myself.

Mum: That's great. _____ (let / have) a look.

Fiona: No, Mum. We _____ (want / do) this by ourselves. Besides, I _____ (call) the landlord an hour ago and he _____ (say) that Tom and I could see the flat next Monday.

Mum: _____ (think) you two _____ (afford / can) the rent?

Fiona: Yes, I _____ (think) so. Our fantastic music is going to make us rich!

Mum: Who will buy all the furniture?

Fiona: Tom and I _____ (work) in the pub for over two years now. We _____ (save) a decent amount and grandpa _____ (give) me £300 for my birthday last July. The award we _____ (receive) _____ (bring) us another £1000.

Mum: Well, I see that you _____ (be all settled) then.

Fiona: Yes, Mum. But please _____ (not / be) sad when I leave home.

19 Das Past Perfect

Das Past Perfect beschreibt eine Handlung der Vergangenheit. Diese war bereits abgeschlossen, als eine zweite (im Past Tense) begann.

→ Alex **had** just **closed** his front door when he realized that he **had left** his keys inside.

Bildung

Past Perfect Simple:
    Subjekt + **had** + **Past Participle**
After I   had   gone   to Bali I went to Peru.

Past Perfect Progressive:
    Subjekt + **had been** + **Grundform** + **ing**
Sue   had been smoking   for 20 years when she finally gave it up.

Übung 1   Vervollständige die Sätze im Past Perfect.

Alex wanted to go to Washington because he _____ (read) so much about it. After he _____ (check) into his hotel he had a look around the city. As soon as Alex _____ (find) the Library of Congress he went in. By nightfall Alex _____ (walk) all over downtown Washington all day, and he was very tired. After he _____ (return) to the hotel his mother called him. She told him that she _____ (visit) Washington D.C. in 1964. Until that year, she said, people who lived in Washington _____ (not / have) the right to vote for the president. As soon as they _____ (finish talking) Alex went to bed. The next day he went to the National Space Museum because his mother _____ (give) him a very interesting book about it. After Alex _____ (see) the stones from the moon, he left for the U.S. Holocaust Memorial Museum. Unfortunately, it _____ (already / close) by the time he got there, and he _____ (forget) to buy a ticket in advance.

42

Übung 2   Finde ein passendes Verb und setze es ins Past Perfect Progressive.

1. The Bartons moved into a big house in Washington last month. They .... in a very small one with only two bedrooms.

2. When I arrived at the Bartons', I was very late. The Bartons were rather annoyed because they .... a long time for me.

3. We .... at the dining room table for ten minutes when we noticed smoke coming out of the kitchen.

4. Pat Barton .... on the phone for at least twenty minutes before she suddenly remembered her cake in the oven.

Übung 3   Übersetze die fehlenden Satzteile ins Englische.

1. ....
(Nachdem der Kongress lange debattiert hatte) about where the capital could be, they decided to build Washington for that purpose.

2. ....
(Nachdem die Bevölkerung auf ca. 800.000 Menschen angewachsen war) people began to think about constructing a subway system.

3. ....
(Nachdem Alex sich einen Stadtplan von Washington gekauft hatte) he started his sightseeing tour.

4. ....
(Als Alex das Lincoln Memorial besichtigt hatte) he went to Capitol Hill.

5. ....
(Nachdem er an einer Führung im Capitol teilgenommen hatte) he went down Pennsylvania Avenue.

6. Before he got into the White House (hatte er sich drei Stunden lang für eine Eintrittskarte ins berühmteste Haus der Welt angestellt.) ....

20. Die Unterscheidung zwischen Simple Past und Past Perfect

In der Vergangenheit spricht man oft über mehrere Geschehnisse. Will man die **Abfolge** von zwei Geschehen in einem Satz ausdrücken, so benutzt man:
- für das, was sich **zuerst** ereignete, das **Past Perfect** und
- für das, was **folgte**, das **Simple Past**.

→ After Lynn **had eaten** three pieces of cake, she **didn't feel** too well.

Übung 1 — Vervollständige das Gespräch zwischen Rory und Lynn.

Rory: Hi, Lynn! I heard you _____ (be) on vacation last week.

Lynn: Hi, Rory! You _____ (hear) right. I was sailing off Cape Cod.

Rory: That sounds great, but _____ (be) you all by yourself?

Lynn: Oh no! My boyfriend _____ (come) me.

Rory: _____ (he / have) time for that? I thought he was preparing for his final exams at the university.

Lynn: Oh, Rory, you _____ (get) it all mixed up. After Bill – that's my boyfriend's name – _____ (pass) all his exams, he _____ (drive) with me from New York to Cape Cod. The journey _____ (take) us almost three days, because our old car _____ (break) down. But as soon as it _____ (repair) by a friendly mechanic, we _____ (be able / continue) our trip to Hyannisport.

Rory: Now, that's interesting. Isn't that the village where John F. Kennedy _____ (own) a summer home?

Lynn: That's right. So after we _____ (rent) a sailing boat we _____ (go) out into the open sea and I _____ (have) the time of my life. The sun _____ (shine), the wind _____ (blow) … Why don't you come with us next time?

Rory: Thanks for the invitation! I'll think about it.

Übung 2   Verbinde jeweils zwei Sätze mit Hilfe des Past Perfect.

1. Lynn and Bill sailed round the Cape. They returned to the harbour to have dinner.

   After ....

   ....

2. They changed their clothes. The two of them went to a luxurious restaurant.

   As soon as ....

   ....

Übung 3   Dolmetsche den Dialog zwischen Bill und Daniel.

Daniel: Hallo Bill, wie geht es dir?

....

Bill: I'm fine, thanks, but my girlfriend is not feeling well.

....

Daniel: Was ist passiert?

....

Bill: Last week we were fishing on the Florida Keys. After we had found a boat to take
         us out into the open sea, we threw out our lines. Suddenly we saw a black
         shadow under the surface of the water.

....

....

....

Daniel: Was ist daran so besonders?

....

Bill: As soon as we had seen it the shadow swam very close to our boat.

....

Daniel: Was war denn das?

....

Bill: It was a huge shark and my girlfriend was so terrified that she went into shock.

....

....

Daniel: Das ist ja schrecklich.

....

21 Die Formen von *to be*

In allen zusammengesetzten Zeiten sowie bei allen Passivformen spielt das Hilfsverb *to be* eine wichtige Rolle. Deshalb sollen die Formen von *to be* hier noch einmal gesondert geübt werden.

Übung 1

Der folgende Text stammt aus einem Reisebericht. Unterstreiche alle Formen von *to be* und ordne sie den unten aufgeführten Zeitformen zu.

Travel in Australia is more than just sun and fun. Until a few years ago there were a lot of tourists who came to Australia only because of the scenery and the kangaroos, but today more and more tourists are in Australia because they want to enjoy the Australian way of life. Says Will van Dam: "This is the second time in my life I have been here, and this is the third time my wife has been in Australia. The first time that I was in Sydney and Adelaide. After I had been in these big cities for more than two weeks I took a wonderful trip in a boat through the waterways of the northern tropics."

1. Present Tense
2. Past Tense
3. Present Perfect
4. Past Perfect

Übung 2

Bilde Fragen, auf die die unterstrichenen Ausdrücke Antwort geben.

1. Brisbane is in <u>Queensland, Australia</u>.

2. <u>Captain Cook</u> was a famous traveller who explored the seas around Australia.

3. People who look for gold in the ground are called <u>gold diggers</u>.

4. <u>Less than 2 per cent</u> of Australia's population are Aboriginals.

5. A plane ticket from Perth to Canberra is <u>$75</u>.

6. <u>In 1998</u> there were 3.8 million visitors in Australia.

46

Übung 3

Deine Schule hat eine E-Mail-Partnerschaft mit einer Schule in Australien angefangen. Deine Partnerin, eine australische Ureinwohnerin, mailt dir zum ersten Mal. Setze die fehlenden Formen von *to be* ein.

Hello, Tanja. My name .... Toolah. I .... an Australian Aboriginal and I .... 13 years old. My home country, Australia, ... very, very big – almost twice as large as Western Europe. My hobbies .... reading and jogging. There .... seven people in my family, three children, four adults and a lot of animals. .... you coloured or .... you a white girl? My brother says that in Germany all the people .... white. .... that right? .... you ever .... to Australia? I .... never .... outside my village which .... in the Northern Territory. Oh no, sorry, that .... wrong. When I .... about five years old, I .... bitten by an emu. An emu .... a big bird, you know. After I .... dizzy for several minutes my mother called the Flying Doctors who flew us to Darwin. My mother and I .... in a hospital in Darwin for two days before we .... allowed to return home. Now I have told you so much about me, please tell me everything there .... to know about you!

Love, Toolah

Übung 4   **Übersetze folgende Sätze.**

1. Es gibt keine Insel, die so groß ist wie Australien.

2. Vor nicht allzu langer Zeit gab es in Australien viele verschiedene Arten von Koalabären.

3. Heutzutage sind die Koalas die Lieblingstiere vieler Touristen.

4. Hat es jemals Flamingos in Australien gegeben?

Unregelmäßige Verben

Übung 1   Finde die richtigen Past Tense-Formen. Die jeweiligen Infinitive findest du unter dem Rätsel.

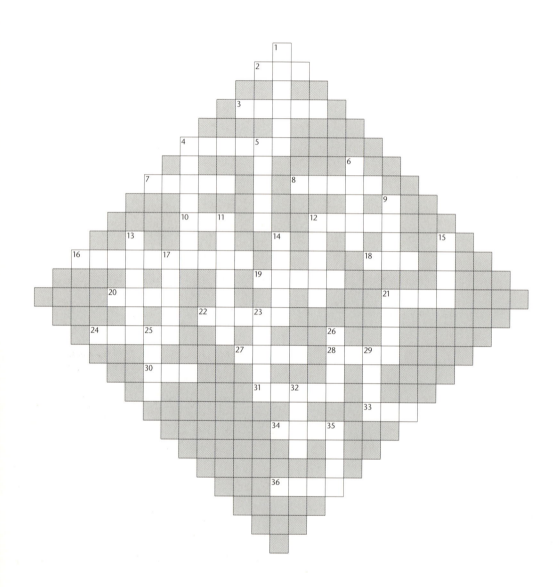

Waagerecht: 2. have, 3. begin, 4. buy, 7. break, 8. write, 10. get, 12. speak, 16. understand, 18. eat, 19. find, 20. come, 21. shut, 22. choose, 24. spell, 27. fall, 28. lose, 30. feed, 31. throw, 33. meet, 34. sing, 36. make

Senkrecht: 1. catch, 4. bring, 5. hear, 6. stand, 9. beat, 11. think, 12. shine, 13. become, 14. drive, 15. go, 17. sleep, 21. send, 23. spend, 25. leave, 26. blow, 29. swim, 32. read, 35. give

Übung 2   Ergänze die fehlenden Formen der unregelmäßigen Verben.

take		
	stole	
	ran	
lose		
	forgot	
		given
cut		
	dug	
		built
	did	
grow		
	knew	
hurt		
		gone
	found	
feel		
		drunk
see		
	left	
hold		
		been
lend		
	sold	
shut		
		shot
	won	
fly		
		taught
ring		
	paid	

49

23   Test zu den bisher geübten Tenses

Übung 1 Die 15-jährige Lucy und ihre gleichaltrige Freundin Claire unterhalten sich in einem New Yorker Café. Setze die Verbformen in der richtigen Zeit ein.

Lucy: Hello, Claire. How _____ (you / be)?

Claire: Fine, thanks. How about yourself?

Lucy: Oh, I _____ (be) okay, but _____ (you / hear) the

latest news about Ralph?

Claire: You _____ (mean) the boy who _____ (come) into our class for the first

time two weeks ago?

Lucy: Yeah, that _____ (be) him. Matt, my boyfriend, _____ (be) at Colthard High

School on 57th Street with him. Guess what he _____ (tell) me about Ralph.

Claire: I _____ (not / have) the slightest idea.

Lucy: They _____ (say) that Ralph _____ (sell) drugs.

Claire: I _____ (not / believe) such nonsense. Ralph _____

(seem) to be such a nice guy. He even _____ (help) me with my maths

homework the other day. I _____ (hate) maths and when I _____ (ask)

him to come over to my house he _____ (agree) at once. Even my

mother _____ (chat) with him a bit. Afterwards she _____ (say),

"What a nice boy. I _____ (hope) you and he _____ (spend)

more time together."

Lucy: Now _____ (listen), Claire. Matt _____ (see) Ralph in a very dangerous

part of New York yesterday. He _____ (talk) to two guys

who _____ (hand) him a couple of dollar bills.

Wenn du mehr über Lucy, Claire, Matt und Ralph wissen möchtest, dann fülle auch noch den Test auf S. 51 aus. Wenn du für heute genug geübt hast, dann rechne deine Note aus:

Für jede richtige Verbform bekommst du 2 Punkte. Bei einem Rechtschreibfehler musst du dir einen halben Punkt wieder abziehen.

50 Punkte – 44 Punkte = Note 1		30,5 Punkte – 24,5 Punkte = Note 4
43,5 Punkte – 37,5 Punkte = Note 2		24 Punkte – 18 Punkte = Note 5
37 Punkte – 31 Punkte = Note 3		ab 17,5 Punkte = Note 6

50

Übung 2

Hier ist die Fortsetzung der Unterhaltung zwischen Lucy und ihrer Freundin Claire. Setze die Verbformen in der richtigen Zeit ein.

Claire: And what .... (happen) then?

Lucy: It .... (be) late at night and Ralph .... (give) the men something Matt .... (not / can / see).

Claire: This .... (sound) unbelievable. And what .... (Matt / do) in a place like that late at night?

Lucy: He and his family .... (drive) home from Broadway, where they .... (see) a wonderful play with Nicole Kidman. And while they .... (go) through this part of town, they .... (see) Ralph standing there dealing drugs.

Claire: Sorry, Lucy, I still .... (not / believe) you.

Lucy: But look, ... (Ralph / come). Hello, Ralph.

Ralph: Hello, you two. Oh, what a night I .... (have) yesterday.

Lucy: We would love to hear about it.

Ralph: Last night, I .... (be) out with my parents. We .... (be) on Broadway watching a wonderful play ...

Lucy: ... with Nicole Kidman.

Ralph: That .... (be) right. We .... (just / walk) home when I suddenly .... (step) on a wallet (dt. Geldbörse). I .... (it / pick up) and .... (find) $1,000 in it. Then we .... (notice) two men who .... (look) for something. It was their wallet, so I .... (return) it to them. I .... (give) a $100 reward.

Claire: Oh Ralph, I .... (be) so glad to hear that. Why .... (you / come) home with me and .... (help) me with my maths? Bye, Lucy!

Notenschlüssel:

52 Punkte – 46 Punkte	= Note 1	31,5 Punkte – 26,5 Punkte = Note 4
45,5 Punkte – 39,5 Punkte	= Note 2	25 Punkte – 19 Punkte = Note 5
38 Punkte – 32 Punkte	= Note 3	ab 18,5 Punkte = full house

24 Übersicht über die Zeiten

Übung 1   Ergänze die fehlenden Zeitformen im Aktiv.

Simple Present	Present Progressive	Simple Past	Present Perfect	Past Perfect
		I accepted		
you rise				
			he has taken	
	she is helping			
				it had declined
		we shared		
you praise				
			they have struck	
		I got to know		
you point				
				he had employed

Übung 2   Ergänze die fehlenden Zeitformen im Passiv.

Simple Present	Present Progressive	Simple Past	Present Perfect	Past Perfect
		I was accepted		
you are shaken				
			he has been taken	
	she is being helped			
				it had been declined
		it was shared		
you are praised				
			they have been elected	
		I was told		
it is pointed out				
				he had been employed

Knaur Verlag München

Englisch 9./10. Klasse

Martina Mattes
Die Zeiten – Bildung und Verwendung

Lösungsteil
(an der Perforation heraustrennen)

Mentor Übungsbuch 852

mentor Verlag München

1. Das Simple Present in Aussagesätzen

Übung 1 Beachte das s in der 3. Person Singular und die Wortstellung (S–P–O)!
1. Before they play golf Nina and George have lunch at 12.30 every day.
2. Nina's handicap is 12, George's handicap is 13.
3. George tries to take part in golf tournaments regularly.
4. Nina sometimes watches (Beachte das e, das nach Zischlauten vor das Präsens-s eingeschoben wird.) Grand Prix racing on TV.
5. She and her friend like car racing but they think it is very dangerous.
6. Ferrari and McLaren are very successful teams in motor sport.

Übung 2 Canoeing and rock-climbing are two of George's leisure activities. He often falls into the water but he can always swim to the bank. Nina and many of her friends are interested in horseback-riding. They have several horses they can ride. 'Black Beauty' is Nina's favourite. It costs a lot of money to own a horse, so Nina works in a fast food restaurant every Saturday. With the money she pays the vet who comes to see 'Black Beauty' regularly.

Übung 3
1. I like to play volleyball and I am very good at (!) this sport.
2. My brother George and I are members of the school team.
3. My big sister Marla hates all kinds of ball games.
4. She is crazy about horses and fast cars.

Übung 4
1. Heißluftballone scheinen jeden zu faszinieren.
2. Ballonfahren ist ein wunderbares, aber auch ein teures Hobby.
   (Beachte: Das englische Wort also heißt in der deutschen Übersetzung auch, das deutsche Wort also heißt im Englischen so oder therefore.)
3. Ein neuer Ballon kann zwischen 15.000 und 45.000 Dollar kosten.
4. Nach einer sicheren Landung trinken der Pilot und seine Passagiere immer ein Glas Sekt.

2. Das Simple Present in Fragesätzen und Verneinungen

Übung 1
1. Do most of the teachers talk too much?
2. The maths teacher does not give homework over the weekend.
3. He does not believe it if anyone tells him that maths is the most difficult subject in the world.

Übung 2
Ralf: Do you go to a girls' school?
Mary: Oh, no, I don't. I go to a comprehensive school in the south of London.
Ralf: I heard that in England a lot of school children have to wear a school uniform but they don't like it. Is that true?
Mary: I am not so sure about that. My school uniform is pretty, but my brother doesn't like his at all.

Übung 3
1. (Does your homework not … klingt bei dieser Unterhaltung ziemlich gestelzt.)
   Doesn't your homework take up most of your afternoon?
2. Don't many of the pupils/students (pupils *im amerikanischen Englisch nur für Grundschüler*) like German literature?
3. Why doesn't the school provide us with free lunch?
   (*Keep in mind: Die Kurzform von* do not *ist* don't, *von* does not *heißt sie* doesn't.)

Übung 4
1. Do many French schoolchildren go to comprehensive schools?
2. I don't think so.
3. Do you know a famous boarding school?
4. Are Winchester and Harrow towns with very expensive schools?
5. Does Prince William go to a school near his grandmother's castle?

Übung 5
1. Ich will nicht über das britische Schulsystem sprechen.
2. Muss dein Vater wirklich Schulgeld für dich zahlen?
3. Haben ihre Lehrer viel Geduld?
4. Laura hat keine Schwierigkeit mit ihrer Englischhausaufgabe.
5. Was hältst du von Peters Einstellung gegenüber Prüfungen?

10 11   **3. Das Present Progressive**

Übung 1
1. Robots are putting together the parts of the cars.
2. Computers are controlling the quality of the work done on the assembly lines.
3. Engineers are checking the amount of time needed by the workers.

Übung 2
1. The Ford company is just modernizing its factory in Detroit.
2. Today the car industry is trying to develop non-polluting cars.
3. New production lines are improving the quality of the new cars.
4. Some factory workers are waiting for the shift to start.
5. Other workers are looking forward to having a break.

Übung 3
Craig: Hi Wayne, I hope I'm not disturbing you at the moment.
Wayne: Well, I'm trying to get some sleep. I was partying all night long.
Craig: And what is your Dad doing?
Wayne: He's working in his garage, I guess. He's probably repairing his old Thunderbird. But why are you calling so early in the morning?
Craig: I'm desperately trying to get some help. My Dad's Porsche is sitting at the bottom of our swimming pool and you or your Dad must help me.
Wayne: What? What are you saying? You're joking, aren't you?
Craig: No, I'm not. I'm dead serious. I was a little drunk last night so I forgot to put on the handbrake and the Porsche slowly rolled down the drive into the swimming pool.
Wayne: Okay, okay, I'm on my way.

Übung 4
While the three men are pulling the Porsche out of the swimming pool, Craig's father comes back from his business trip. When he sees what is going on he has a heart attack. Craig helps his father until the ambulance arrives. While they are hurrying to the hospital, Craig worries about what will happen. Fortunately, the driver is driving fast so that they reach the hospital in time. While Craig's father is recovering from his shock, Craig and Wayne have the Porsche repaired. When Craig's father sees his Porsche again it is shining like new.

58   Lösungen

4. Die Unterscheidung zwischen Simple Present und Present Progressive

Übung 1

Cory: Can you hear those girls over there? Are they talking about us?
Alison: I don't think so but maybe it is a good idea to leave the party now. What do you think?
Cory: I'm not sure. I usually really enjoy parties but I'm not enjoying this one. The boys here are a bit shy, and the other girls …
Alison: Why don't we leave and go to my brother's party? He's having one right now in his beautiful apartment in Kensington.
Cory: I don't like the idea.
Alison: Oh, come on. Don't be (*Vorsicht: Hier ist* to be *ein Vollverb und muss mit* to do *bei der Verneinung umschrieben werden.*) such a spoilsport!
Cory: All right, then. But first I must call my parents. They always want to know where I am. I wonder what they are doing at the moment. I hope they are not waiting for me.
Alison: Oh, you and your parents. Mine are much less complicated. They don't care what I'm doing as long as it's not illegal and I come home every night.
Cory: Okay, let's go! But lend me your mobile phone first, please.

Übung 2

Signalwörter für das Simple Present: usually, always, every day.
Signalwörter für das Present Progressive: right now, at the moment.
Weitere Signalwörter für das Simple Present: sometimes, regularly, occasionally, often, seldom.
Weitere Signalwörter für das Present Progressive: look!, listen!, still, just.

Übung 3

1. Hey you. What are you staring at ~~do you stare at~~?
2. Why are you driving ~~do you drive~~ so fast? – Because we are late.
3. Can I turn the CD-player down? You are not listening ~~do not listen~~ anyway.
4. What are you eating ~~do you eat~~? – I'm having a piece of cake.
5. Are you Swedish? – No, ~~I'm coming~~ I come from Denmark.
6. How many languages do you speak ~~are you speaking~~?
7. When does school usually start ~~is school usually starting~~ in Denmark?
8. What are you doing ~~do you do~~ right now? – Are you blind? I am playing ~~I play~~ cards with Joe.

Übung 4

Alison: Oh, I love this party. The people here are so cool.
Cory: Look! Isn't that Elton John over there?
Alison: Listen! He is singing his latest song with the Spice Girls. And look over there! Mick Jagger is kissing a blonde lady.
Cory: Wow, and what is your brother doing? He is holding hands with Tina Turner.
Alison: If I weren't / wasn't seeing this with my own eyes, I wouldn't believe it.

5. Das Passiv im Present Tense

Übung 1

find, found, found
join, joined, joined
catch, caught, caught
be, was/were, been

drill, drilled, drilled
drink, drank, drunk
build, built, built

Übung 2

1. A lot of birds and animals are killed.
2. Men on special ships are hired for that.
3. Yes, tankers are used to bring oil on shore.
4. Radios are often not switched off and lights are left on.

Übung 3

1. Lots of workers are needed for the work on the platforms.
2. High wages are paid by the oil companies.
3. The platform cannot be left by the workers unless they have permission from their boss.
4. In bad weather or in a heavy storm the men working on the platform are tossed around.

Übung 4

John: Ich muss gezwungenermaßen (bin gezwungen) noch mindestens zwei Monate an diesem unfreundlichen Ort (zu) bleiben.
Heinz: That is really bad.
John: Ich bin als Taucher eingestellt worden und ich bin der Einzige hier an Bord, der tauchen kann.
Heinz: But can't you just leave?
John: Nein, das ist unmöglich. Aber meine Tage hier sind gezählt, glaube mir.

Übung 5

1. Smoking is not allowed on an oil rig.
2. How is petrol (gas = am. engl.) produced from crude oil?
3. New oil fields can still be found nowadays.
4. Alcohol is not allowed on oil rigs. / Drinking alcohol is not allowed on oil rigs.

6. Mixed Exercises zum Present Tense

Übung 1

John Taylor is an English engineer. He specializes in drilling for oil in the North Sea. This year he is working on an oil rig, which is called 'Blet Sar'. He does not speak any Norwegian, but he is trying to learn at least some of the most important words. John knows that he earns / is earning good money but he misses his wife and four children very much. He usually likes his work, but at the moment it is raining heavily and no work can be done on the oil rig. Right now John and his Norwegian friends are playing Monopoly so that they do not feel lonely.

Übung 2

Dear Daddy,
I miss you so much. Life is boring without you. Do you like your job in the North Sea? I hate it because it takes you away from me. While I am writing this, I am crying the whole time. I feel / am feeling so lonely at the moment. Sorry that the letter has so many watery spots. These are my tears. Please, Daddy, come back soon!
Lots of love, Priscilla
P.S. Mummy wants me to say hello to you for her.

Übung 3

1. Sometimes children are talked to as if they are stupid.
2. Do you think these kids are capable of doing it all by themselves?
3. The young people of today do not feel miserable because they believe they will have a wonderful future.
4. Boys and girls have equal educational opportunities, as is required by law.
5. It is not reasonable for girls to be refused *(Infinitiv Passiv! refuse heißt (ver)weigern: den Mädchen wird / ist das Betreten verboten)* entry into an all-male club.

Übung 4

1. A lot of pupils *(brit. engl.)* / students *(am. engl.)* in German grammar schools / high schools think that speaking English as the English do is difficult.
2. There are a lot of words the pupils have never heard of.
3. During the test most of the pupils wish that they had studied more.
4. It is generally known that English is one of the easiest languages in the world.
5. Do you know how many people in the world speak English?
6. In almost every continent there is at least one nation whose mother tongue is English.
7. English is spoken all over the world.
8. Do you like the English language?

7. Das Simple Past

Übung 1
1. The lady got up at six o'clock in the morning.
2. She had a shower and had breakfast.
3. She drank tea and ate toast with butter.
4. Every morning a friend stopped (*Beachte:* to stop, *aber* stopped; *die Regel lautet: Nach kurzem, einfachem, betontem Vokal wird der Endkonsonant vor* -ed *verdoppelt.*) in front of her house and took her to work.

Übung 2
1. How long did you stay in the United States?
2. Did you like it there?
3. How many new friends did you make?

Übung 3
Last month I went to the unemployment office. They offered me a job and I accepted it at once. I was unemployed for several months but now I am working as a waitress. Last week I got my first pay cheque. Yesterday I spent it all on beautiful clothes. I bought a blue dress, a green T-shirt and a really great skirt. I paid $45. Yesterday was a wonderful day.

Übung 4
1. In 1998 I worked as an au pair in New York for one year.
2. I didn't like it there.
3. The family I worked for lived on a very noisy street in Manhattan.
4. I was glad when the year was over.

Übung 5
1. Where did you work in 1998?
2. Did you like it in New York?
3. What was the weather like?
4. How did you get on with the family?

62 Lösungen

8. Das Past Progressive

Übung 1
1. At 6.03 o'clock she was taking a shower.
2. At 6.16 o'clock she was getting dressed.
3. At 6.37 o'clock she was running to the train station.
4. At 7 o'clock she was sitting in the train.

Übung 2
1. Diana was standing in the shower when the lights went out.
2. She was putting on her new blouse when a button came off.
3. Diana was having breakfast when the telephone rang.
4. She was leaving the house when she heard a shout.

Übung 3
1. Sylvia was talking on the phone while the earth was shaking.
2. Sylvia's father was staring out of the hotel window as the Bay Bridge was collapsing.
3. Two men were trying to steal expensive diamonds while the owner was having dinner in the hotel restaurant.

Übung 4
Sylvia: The floor was shaking and we realized that it was an earthquake.
Diana: Was hast du / habt ihr (da) gerade gemacht?
Sylvia: My brother and my sister were playing chess, my mother was writing her novel and I was bathing the dog.
Diana: Das klingt unglaublich. Hast du wirklich während eines Erdbebens den Hund gebadet?
Sylvia: Yes, I was. But the dog went crazy. After the earthquake he was hiding / hid under my bed all night long.

Lösungen 63

9. Die Unterscheidung zwischen Simple Past und Past Progressive

Übung 1
1. What were you doing this time yesterday?
2. I was packing my suitcase for our trip to Wales, and …
3. … my sister Friederike was surfing the Internet for infos about Cardiff.
4. Did she find anything?
5. No, she didn't. (Nur mit "No!" zu antworten ist sehr unhöflich und deshalb nicht akzeptabel.) She was just chatting with a Welshman when her computer crashed.

Übung 2
While we were heading for Wales, my brother was travelling (brit. engl.) / traveling (am. engl.) to Scotland. He wanted to climb Ben Nevis, the highest mountain in Scotland. But while he was climbing Ben Nevis some rocks kept falling down. Fortunately, nobody was hurt.

Übung 3
Helen: Did you have a nice holiday?
Sue: Oh yeah. It was great.
Helen: Where were you exactly?
Sue: First we went by plane to London, then we rented a car and drove to Cymru the same day.
Helen: What did you say?
Sue: We travelled (brit. engl.) / traveled (am. engl.) to Wales, which is called Cymru in Welsh. We stayed in a haunted castle with lots of ghosts. When they were rattling their chains, nobody could sleep. Old Faithful, one of the ghosts, was just following me, when he dropped his head. Another one was coming after my little sister when he fell over a big wooden chest.
Helen: Weren't you afraid?
Sue: No, I wasn't. I had a lot of fun.

Übung 4
1. When the clock struck 12, we were lying in our beds.
2. Plötzlich öffnete sich die Tür.
3. A ghost with his head under his arm was slowly entering the room.
4. Ich schaltete das Licht an und die Kreatur verschwand für immer.
5. The next night we were able to sleep safe and sound.

10. Das Passiv im Past Tense

Übung 1

When I was seven years old, I was allowed to go to school for the first time in my life. My brothers and I went to a building that was built by white settlers. At the door we were welcomed by a nice young woman who was called "Madame" by the other schoolchildren. I was very excited and I liked school a lot. One day, as our maths tests were just being returned, there was a terrible noise outside. After a while the sound could not be heard any more. Then there it was again. Suddenly the door was opened wide by a big grizzly. Another big roar was heard, and then there was a shot. Our teacher was standing there with a gun in her hands. The animal was shot by our brave schoolteacher. We were each allowed to take a tooth from the bear. I will remember this incident and this woman all my life.

Übung 2
1. When was "Flying Arrow" sent to school?
2. By whom was the school built? / Who was the school built by?
3. By whom was he taught? / Who was he taught by? *(Oder am besten:* Who was his teacher?*)*
4. What was his teacher called?
5. Which animal were the lessons disturbed by one day?
6. Which tests were being returned when the bear came in?
7. Who was the grizzly shot by?
8. Who was allowed to keep the teeth?
9. When was this adventure told?
10. Who was this story told by? / By whom was this story told?

Übung 3
1. A lot of old stories were told to my brothers and sisters and me.
2. One story was especially loved by all of us.
3. It was the story of the Red Indian called "Eagle Eye" who was raised and fed by a wolf.

Lösungen 65

11. Mixed Exercises zum Past Tense

Übung 1

1. Bill Gates was born in Seattle, Washington, in the year 1955.
2. At the age of 12 he was already fascinated by computers.
3. In 1975 Bill Gates and his partner Paul Allen developed a computer-programming language called BASIC.
4. In the same year Bill Gates left Harvard University to have more time for his company, Microsoft.
5. In 1989 the Corbis Corporation was founded by Gates.
6. Six years later this company bought 16 million photographic images and plans were announced to digitize a lot of them.

Übung 2

1. Yesterday Tom was writing on his computer when it suddenly crashed.
2. He called his friend Celine who promised to come to his house immediately.
3. After a couple of minutes the error / bug was found by Celine.
4. They were playing on the computer when a loud shout was heard.
5. Tom's mother was also having trouble with her computer.
6. Tom's mother could be helped by Celine, too.

Übung 3

Celine: Hi, Tom. How did it go in yesterday's exam?
Tom: Well, in the beginning I thought that I had all the right answers but then I saw what the others had written and now I know that I might have failed.
Celine: Did you revise enough?
Tom: Oh yes, I think so. My mother helped me a lot and even my Dad studied with me. He listened for over two hours to what I told him about the Boston Tea Party and its consequences. But what about you?
Celine: I think I did alright. In the exam I was asked about Thanksgiving and I was able to tell the teachers a lot. They were quite pleased with me.
Tom: You lucky girl. Why wasn't I asked by my teachers about easy stuff like Thanksgiving? I would have known almost everything about that, but in my exam I could remember almost nothing about a war that took place more than 200 years ago.
Celine: If I were you, I wouldn't worry too much. I'm sure you will pass the exam. By the way, did you and your friends celebrate the end of the schoolyear yesterday?
Tom: Yes, we did. We partied all night long. Why weren't you there?
Celine: I wasn't there because I wasn't invited.
Tom: Oh, Celine! I'm so sorry.

Lösungen

12. Das Present Perfect Simple in Aussagesätzen

Übung 1
1. Aunt Margie has tried to call us from Boston several times today.
2. She has not seen us since 1985.

Übung 2
1. We have never had guests from America before.
2. We have invited Aunt Margie several times.
3. But this is the first time she has accepted our invitation.
4. Aunt Margie has lived on the East Coast all her life.
5. She has never visited Germany before.
6. The weather in Boston has been terrible for over a week now.
7. Aunt Margie has known us since we were babies.

Übung 3
1. The children have finally seen their aunt again.
2. She has brought along a book about Boston.
3. Margie has been to Europe thirteen times so far.
4. She has seen a lot of cities and countries.
5. She has played now with the Boston Philharmonic for 20 years.
6. Her brother has conducted the Boston Pops since 1989.
7. We have tried to get tickets for the festival, but so far we have not succeeded.

Übung 4
1. Ich habe die Biografie über John F. Kennedy gelesen, der in Boston geboren wurde.
2. Bis jetzt waren wir noch nie in Kanada, aber wir sind beinahe in jedem Staat der USA gewesen.
3. Sarah ist jetzt seit fünf Monaten Touristenführerin in Boston.
4. Bist du jemals dem Pfad der Freiheit im Stadtzentrum von Boston gefolgt?

Lösungen

13. Das Present Perfect in Frage und Verneinung

Übung 1

Suzi has not been in Salzburg for six months. Her boyfriend has been a skiing instructor since he was 19 years old. Because there are so many people who want to take skiing lessons, she has not seen him since November, but today is his day off and he and Suzi have been skiing for at least four hours. Now they are very tired. They go back to the hotel-room where Suzi has been staying for more than a week now. She turns on her lap-top and goes online, but nobody has mailed her since yesterday. Suddenly his mobile phone (*brit. engl.; am. engl.:* cell phone) rings and somebody says that there has been a terrible accident in the mountains. Four people have been buried under masses of snow for a quarter of an hour. This is the worst accident since 1998 when two teenagers were missing for more than three days.

Übung 2

1. How many times have you been to Austria before?
2. Has one of your students ever had an accident?
3. How long have you been a skiing instructor?
4. Have you earned a lot of money so far?

Übung 3

1. Have you ever thought of spending your holiday in our lovely town?
2. We bet you've never seen a more beautiful sunset in the mountains!
3. And why haven't you tried our world-famous dumplings yet?
4. Our guests have never complained about long queues at the ski-lifts!
5. And they haven't paid high prices here either!

Übung 4

N: Joe went skiing two days ago. Have you heard from him so far?
L: No, I have not seen him since last Friday.
N: He wanted to call me, but he has not done so yet.
L: Don't worry too much. I have known Joe for ages and he has never kept his promises.
N: I heard on the news this morning that the weather has changed in the place where he has been staying for two days now.
L: All right then. I have the number of his mobile phone. Let's call him.

68 Lösungen

14. Das Present Perfect Progressive

Übung 1
1. Ich schaue die königliche Hochzeit jetzt schon seit zwei Stunden an.
2. Die Sonne scheint schon seit dem Beginn der Hochzeit.
3. Der Prinz starrt seine Braut an, seitdem sie die Kirche betrat.
4. Die Königinmutter weint, seitdem das Paar die Ringe tauschte.

Übung 2
Ute: Hey, Tony, you look tired. Have you been working hard the last few days?
Tony: Oh no. Quite the opposite. I have just arrived from Los Angeles. It was wonderful over there. I was visiting my big sister. She is a famous actress. She has appeared in several films.
Ute: Wow, I'm impressed. It has always been my dream to go there and become a star. How often have you been to L.A.?
Tony: I have been there twice. I just came back this morning. By the way, I have been reading the book you gave me months ago, but I have not finished it yet.
Ute: You can keep it. But let's talk about your sister. How long has she been living in California?
Tony: Suzanne – that's my sister's name – has been living in Beverly Hills for more than five years now. Her husband founded a big studio and he has successfully headed it for a long time now. When I was visiting them he even offered me a small part in the latest movie with Julia Roberts.
Ute: This is hard to believe.
Tony: No, seriously. I have been taking dance lessons since I was five. For 15 years now I have been dancing every Friday and Saturday. I am a very good dancer. I have just won the national championship for the third time. Don't you believe me?
Ute: Oh, come on. Have you really been dancing for such a long time?
Tony: Yeah, sure. Let's dance, and I'll show you!

Lösungen 69

15. Das Passiv im Present Perfect

Übung 1
1. Up to now Universal Studios have been visited by millions of people.
2. More science fiction movies than love stories have been shown in recent years.
3. How many films have been directed by Steven Spielberg so far?
4. Why has Tom Cruise not been awarded an Oscar yet?
5. So far the latest James Bond movie has been seen by over 2,000,000 people.
6. Hundreds of thousands of young actors have been attracted by Hollywood over the years.

Übung 2
1. A new cinema has just been opened in Hatfield.
2. The new film has been talked about for weeks now.
3. The actress Meg Ryan has been fired and Julia Roberts has been hired instead. Since then not a word has been exchanged between the two ladies.
4. Have the rights to the film been sold to other countries yet?
5. At least 100 cars have been destroyed so far during the filming of the new James Bond movie.
6. Have you ever been invited to a film premiere?

Übung 3
1. She has never be seen in a cowboy film before.
   She has never been seen in a cowboy film before.
2. These horses have not been yet trained.
   These horses have not been trained yet.
3. Hugh Grant's last film have been in production for over nine months now.
   Hugh Grant's last film has been in production for over nine months now.
4. It has been directed of a very famous woman.
   It has been directed by a very famous woman.

Übung 4
1. Spielberg's latest film has been described as "excellent".
2. This film has been nominated for six Oscars.

Lösungen

16. Die Unterscheidung zwischen Past Tense und Present Perfect

Übung 1

Robin Hood was once a rich man, but he had lost all his money.
He and his men lived of the rich people who passed by.
His best friend was called Little John.
The outlaws never robbed or hurt the poor and needy.
His men wore green so that it was difficult to see them in the forest.
They never kept the stolen things for themselves.
Maid Marian was married to Robin Hood.
Robin and his men liked to hunt and fish in Sherwood Forest.
Have you ever seen Kevin Costner as Robin Hood?

Übung 2

1. Have you ever heard of Robin Hood?
2. He was a brave and noble man who fought for the poor.
3. In Sherwood Forest there was a camp where all the outlaws lived at that time.
4. Was *(Passiv!)* Robin loved by everyone?
5. Why did Robin Hood steal money from the rich?

Übung 3

1. I ~~did~~ not see a film about Robin Hood in years. I have not seen a film about Robin Hood in years. 2. Robin Hood's life ~~was~~ filmed about 20 times so far. Robin Hood's life has been filmed about 20 times so far. 3. Friar Tuck and Little John ~~have~~ always accompanied Robin. Friar Tuck and Little John always accompanied Robin. 4. The merry man of Nottingham ~~has~~ loved his wife madly. The merry man of Nottingham loved his wife madly. 5. In the 14th century Edward II ~~has been~~ King of England. In the 14th century Edward II was King of England. 6. Have you seen Robin Hood's statue in Nottingham? *(Das Present Perfect ist hier genauso richtig wie das Past Tense:* Did you see Robin Hood's statue in Nottingham?*)*

Übung 4

One day when Robin Hood was riding with Little John through Sherwood Forest they heard loud voices. They came closer and saw two ladies on white horses. The women were surrounded *(Passiv!)* by three soldiers who had swords in their hands. "Go away!" one of the ladies shouted. "We have been on our horses for more than two hours and we don't want to return to where we came from. Let us pass!" But the soldiers did not allow them to continue their ride through the forest. Robin and Little John fought with the soldiers, defeated them and rescued the two ladies. These two women gave Robin a golden ring as a gift because they were so grateful. In those days a lot of people worshipped Robin Hood and thought he was a great hero.

Lösungen

17. Past Tense oder Present Perfect?

Übung 1

Frank: Hi, Karen, we haven't seen each other for a long time.
Karen: Yes, you're right. The last time we met was at my sister's birthday party last September.
Frank: That's right. I even remember the topic we were talking *(oder auch möglich: talked)* about.
Karen: What was it? I can't remember.
Frank: Robin Hood and his life in the Middle Ages.
Karen: When did you hear about him for the first time?
Frank: I heard about Robin Hood in kindergarten. Our teacher taught us a song about Robin and Maid Marian and since then I have read a lot about him.
Karen: Did you know that his father was a brave knight?
Frank: Is that true?
Karen: About 100 years ago people didn't know exactly where his place of birth was but then they found his grave in Nottingham.
Frank: No, that's not true. I read in the newspaper only last week that his grave has not been found *(Passiv)* yet, and that they are still looking for it.
Karen: Do you know whether the Sheriff of Nottingham ever caught Robin?
Frank: Yes, I do. I heard in the news only a couple of days ago that the Sheriff could never get hold of Robin.

Übung 2

Mark: Hello, Sue. This is Mark. Have you finished your homework yet?
Sue: Yes, I have. It was very difficult to write a dialogue between Robin Hood and the Sheriff of Nottingham. At first I didn't know what I should write about them, but then my little brother came into my room and disturbed me and suddenly I knew what the two were saying to each other.
Mark: You're lucky. Yesterday I was in the public library and I found a very interesting book there on the Romans and the Saxons. Unfortunately it didn't say a single word about Robin Hood. Now I have been thinking about this stupid dialogue for hours and my mind is blank.
Sue: Don't give up, Mark. I'll help you.
Mark: That's very kind of you. I have already written the beginning of the conversation. Listen, please, and tell me, whether you like it or not. "On October 14th, 1066, Duke William of Normandy met and defeated the English army at Hastings, where he killed King Harold. On Christmas Day a bishop crowned him in Westminster Abbey. From then on his new name was William I. Later he became known as William the Conqueror."
Sue: That's very interesting but you haven't mentioned one single word about Robin so far, have you?
Mark: Oh, Sue, you're very impatient. I told you just a couple of minutes ago that this dialogue is terribly hard for me.
Sue: Well, why don't you come to my house and we'll do your homework together.
Mark: That sounds wonderful. Thank you so much. I'll be over in a sec.

72 Lösungen

18. Mixed Exercises

Übung 1

When Tom was a bit younger, he used to do a lot of sports, but now he has no time for that because every other night he plays in a band in his hometown of Liverpool. The band is called the "Easy Beets". Besides Tom there are William, the guitarist, James, who plays the piano, and Tom's girlfriend Fiona, who sings and writes beautiful songs about life and love. The three are so successful that last year they even won a music contest. The best music group was given a gold medal by Paul McCartney, who is one of the most famous pop stars in the world.

Übung 2

1. Liverpool has always offered young musicians the opportunity to play in front of an audience.
2. Eight years ago the first music competition for talented teenagers took place.
3. There are some bands whose career started in a pub years ago.
4. Of course all the young musicians want to get record contracts.
5. But most of them are making music simply because they enjoy it very much.

Übung 3

Fiona: Mum, I'm going to wash the dishes now.
Mum: That's okay, Fiona. I have already done it. Are you going to see Grandpa tonight?
Fiona: No, I saw him yesterday.
Mum: Fiona, have you read today's newspaper yet?
Fiona: Yes, I have and it seems as if I have found an apartment for Tom and myself.
Mum: That's great. Let me have a look.
Fiona: No, Mum. We want to do this by ourselves. Besides, I called the landlord an hour ago and he said that Tom and I could see the flat next Monday.
Mum: Do you think you two can afford the rent?
Fiona: Yes, I think so. Our fantastic music is going to make us rich.
Mum: Who will buy all the furniture?
Fiona: Tom and I have been working in the pub for over two years now. We have saved a decent amount and grandpa gave me £300 for my birthday last July. The award we received brought us another £1000.
Mum: Well, I see that you are all settled then.
Fiona: Yes, Mum. But please, don't be *(Die verneinte Befehlsform von be heißt don't be – sei nicht.)* sad when I leave home.

Lösungen 73

19. Das Past Perfect

Übung 1

Alex wanted to go to Washington because he had read so much about it. After he had checked into his hotel he had a look around the city. As soon as Alex had found the Library of Congress he went in. By nightfall Alex had been walking all over downtown Washington all day, and he was very tired. After he had returned to the hotel his mother called him. She told him that she had visited Washington D.C. in 1964. Until that year, she said, people who lived in Washington had not had the right to vote for the president. As soon as they had finished talking Alex went to bed. The next day he went to the National Space Museum because his mother had given him a very interesting book about it. After Alex had seen the stones from the moon, he left for the U.S. Holocaust Memorial Museum. Unfortunately, it had already closed by the time he got there, and he had forgotten to buy a ticket in advance.

Übung 2

1. The Bartons moved into a big house in Washington last month. They had been living in a very small one with only two bedrooms.
2. When I arrived at the Bartons', I was very late. The Bartons were rather annoyed because they had been waiting a long time for me.
3. We had been sitting at the dining room table for ten minutes when we noticed smoke coming out of the kitchen.
4. Pat Barton had been talking on the phone for at least twenty minutes before she suddenly remembered her cake in the oven.

Übung 3

1. After the Congress had argued for a long time ...
2. After the population had grown to about 800,000 people ...
3. After Alex had bought a map of Washington ...
4. When Alex had visited the Lincoln Memorial ...
5. After he had taken part in a guided tour of the Capitol ...
6. Before he got into the White House he had been queuing *(brit. engl.)* / standing in line *(am. engl.)* for three hours to get a ticket to the most famous house in the world.

74 Lösungen

20. Die Unterscheidung zwischen Simple Past und Past Perfect

Übung 1

Rory: Hi, Lynn! I heard you were on vacation *(am. engl.)* / holiday *(brit. engl.)* last week.
Lynn: Hi, Rory! You heard right. I was sailing off Cape Cod.
Rory: That sounds great, but were you all by yourself?
Lynn: Oh no! My boyfriend came with me.
Rory: Did he have time for that? I thought he was preparing for his final exams at the university.
Lynn: Oh Rory, you got it all mixed up. After Bill – that's my boyfriend's name – had passed all his exams, he drove with me from New York to Cape Cod. The journey took us almost three days, because our old car broke down. But as soon as it had been repaired by a friendly mechanic we were able to continue our trip to Hyannisport.
Rory: Now, that's interesting. Isn't that the village where John F. Kennedy owned a summer home?
Lynn: That's right. So after we had rented a sailing boat *(brit. engl.)* / sail boat *(am. engl.)* we went out into the open sea and I had the time of my life. The sun was shining, the wind was blowing … Why don't you come with us next time?
Rory: Thanks for the invitation! I'll think about it.

Übung 2

1. After Lynn and Bill had sailed round the Cape they returned to the harbour to have dinner.
2. As soon as they had changed their clothes the two of them went to a luxurious restaurant.

Übung 3

Daniel: Hello, Bill, how are you?
Bill: Danke, mir geht es gut, aber meine Freundin fühlt sich nicht wohl / gut.
Daniel: What happened? (*Oder:* What's wrong / what's the matter?)
Bill: Letzte Woche waren wir auf den Florida Keys fischen. Nachdem wir ein Boot gefunden hatten, das uns aufs offene Meer hinausbrachte, warfen wir unsere Angeln aus. Plötzlich sahen wir einen schwarzen Schatten unter der Wasseroberfläche.
Daniel: What's so special about that?
Bill: Sobald wir ihn gesehen hatten, schwamm der Schatten ganz nahe an unser Boot heran.
Daniel: What was it then?
Bill: Es war ein riesiger Hai und meine Freundin erschrak so, dass sie einen Schock bekam.
Daniel: That's terrible.

21. Die Formen von *to be*

Übung 1

Travel in Australia is more than just sun and fun. Until a few years ago there were a lot of tourists who came to Australia only because of the scenery and the kangaroos, but today more and more tourists are in Australia because they want to enjoy the Australian way of life. Says Will van Dam: "This is the second time in my life I have been here, and this is the third time my wife has been in Australia. The first time that I was in Sydney and Adelaide. After I had been in these big cities for more than two weeks I took a wonderful trip in a boat through the waterways of the northern tropics."

1. Present Tense: is, are
2. Past Tense: was, were
3. Present Perfect: have been, has been
4. Past Perfect: had been

Übung 2

1. Where is Brisbane?
2. Who was a famous traveller who explored the seas around Australia?
3. What are people called who look for gold in the ground?
4. What percentage of Australia's population are Aboriginals?
5. How much is a plane ticket from Perth to Canberra?
6. In which year were there 3.8 million visitors in Australia?

Übung 3

Hello Tanja. My name is Toolah. I am an Australian Aboriginal and I am 13 years old. My home country, Australia, is very, very big – almost twice as large as Western Europe. My hobbies are reading and jogging. There are seven people in my family, three children, four adults and a lot of animals. Are you coloured or are you a white girl? My brother says that in Germany all the people are white. Is that right? Have you ever been to Australia? I have never been outside my village which is in the Northern Territory. Oh no, sorry, that is wrong. When I was about five years old, I was bitten by an emu. An emu is a big bird, you know. After I had been dizzy for several minutes my mother called the Flying Doctors who flew us to Darwin. My mother and I were in a hospital in Darwin for two days before we were allowed to return home. Now I have told you so much about me, please me everything there is to know about you.

Übung 4

1. There is no island as big as Australia.
2. Not too long ago there were many different kinds of koala bears in Australia.
3. Today koala bears are many tourists' favourite *(brit. engl.)* / favorite *(am. engl.)* pets.
4. Have there ever been flamingos in Australia?

22. Unregelmäßige Verben

Übung 1 Waagerecht: 2. had, 3. began, 4. bought, 7. broke, 8. wrote, 10. got, 12. spoke, 16. understood, 18. ate, 19. found, 20. came, 21. shut, 22. chose, 24. spelt, 27. fell, 28. lost, 30. fed, 31. threw, 33. met, 34. sang, 36. made

Senkrecht: 1. caught, 4. brought, 5. heard, 6. stood, 9. beat, 11. thought, 12. shone, 13. became, 14. drove, 15. went, 17. slept, 21. sent, 23. spent, 25. left, 26. blew, 29. swam, 32. read, 35. gave

Übung 2

take	took	taken
steal	stole	stolen
run	ran	run
lose	lost	lost
forget	forgot	forgotten
give	gave	given
cut	cut	cut
dig	dug	dug
build	built	built
do	did	done
grow	grew	grown
know	knew	known
hurt	hurt	hurt
go	went	gone
find	found	found
feel	felt	felt
drink	drank	drunk
see	saw	seen
leave	left	left
hold	held	held
be	was/were	been
lend	lent	lent
sell	sold	sold
shut	shut	shut
shoot	shot	shot
win	won	won
fly	flew	flown
teach	taught	taught
ring	rang	rung
pay	paid	paid

Lösungen

23. Test zu den bisher geübten Tenses

Übung 1

Lucy: Hello, Claire. How are you?
Claire: Fine, thanks. How about yourself?
Lucy: Oh, I'm okay, but have you heard the latest news about Ralph?
Claire: You mean the boy who came into our class for the first time two weeks ago?
Lucy: Yeah, that's him. Matt, my boyfriend, was at Colthard High School on 57th Street with him. And guess what he told me about Ralph.
Claire: I don't have the slightest idea.
Lucy: They say that Ralph is selling / sells drugs.
Claire: I don't believe such nonsense. Ralph seems to be such a nice guy. He even helped me with my maths homework the other day. I hate maths and when I asked him to come over to my house he agreed at once. Even my mother chatted with him a bit. Afterwards she said, "What a nice boy. I hope you and he will spend more time together."
Lucy: Now listen, Claire. Matt saw Ralph in a very dangerous part of New York yesterday. He was talking to two guys who handed him a couple of dollarbills.

Übung 2

Claire: And what happened then?
Lucy: It was late at night and Ralph gave the men something Matt couldn't see.
Claire: This sounds unbelievable. And what was Matt doing in a place like that late at night?
Lucy: He and his family were driving home from Broadway, where they had seen a wonderful play with Nicole Kidman. And while they were going through this part of town they saw Ralph standing there dealing drugs.
Claire: Sorry, Lucy, I still don't believe you.
Lucy: But look, Ralph is coming. Hello, Ralph.
Ralph: Hello, you two. Oh, what a night I had yesterday.
Lucy: We would love to hear about it.
Ralph: Last night, I was out with my parents. We were on Broadway watching a wonderful play …
Lucy: … with Nicole Kidman.
Ralph: That's right. We were just walking home when I suddenly stepped on a wallet. I picked it up and found $1,000 in it. Then we noticed two men who were looking for something. It was their wallet, so I returned it to them. I was given a $100 reward.
Claire: Oh Ralph, I'm so glad to hear that. Why don't you come home with me and help me with my maths? Bye, Lucy!

Lösungen

24. Übersicht über die Zeiten

Übung 1

Simple Present	Present Progressive	Simple Past	Present Perfect	Past Perfect
Infinitiv oder bei *he/she it* + s	*am/are/is* + Verb + *ing*	2. Form oder Verb + *-ed*	*have/has* + Past Participle	*had* + Past Participle
I accept	I am accepting	I accepted	I have accepted	I had accepted
you rise	you are rising	you rose	you have risen	you had risen
he takes	he is taking	he took	he has taken	he had taken
she helps	she is helping	she helped	she has helped	she had helped
it declines	it is declining	it declined	it has declined	it had declined
we share	we are sharing	we shared	we have shared	we had shared
you praise	you are praising	you praised	you have praised	you had praised
they strike	they are striking	they struck	they have struck	they had struck
I get to know	I am getting to know	I got to know	I have got to know	I had got to know
you point	you are pointing	you pointed	you have pointed	you had pointed
he employs	he is employing	he employed	he has employed	he had employed

Übung 2

Simple Present	Present Progressive	Simple Past	Present Perfect	Past Perfect
am/are/is + Past Participle	*am/are/is* + *being* + Past Participle	*was/were* + Past Participle	*have/has* + *been* + Past Participle	*had* + *been* + Past Participle
I am accepted	I am being accepted	I was accepted	I have been accepted	I had been accepted
you are shaken	you are being shaken	he was shaken	he has been shaken	he had been shaken
he is taken	he is being taken	he was taken	he has been taken	he had been taken
she is helped	she is being helped	she was helped	she has been helped	she had been helped
it is declined	it is being declined	it was declined	it has been declined	it had been declined
it is shared	it is being shared	it was shared	it has been shared	it had been shared
you are praised	you are being praised	you were praised	you have been praised	you had been praised
they are elected	they are being elected	they were elected	they have been elected	they had been elected
I am told	I am being told	I was told	I have been told	I had been told
it is pointed out	it is being pointed out	it was pointed out	it has been pointed out	it had been pointed out
he is employed	he is being employed	he was employed	he has been employed	he had been employed

Lösungen

Mentor Übungsbücher NEU

Das Last-Minute-Programm vor der Klassenarbeit

Deutsch

Diktate leicht gemacht
5. Klasse
ISBN 3-580-63810-6

Diktate leicht gemacht
6. Klasse
ISBN 3-580-63811-4

Aufsatz: Inhaltsangabe
7./8. Klasse
ISBN 3-580-63801-7

**Rechtschreibung:
Groß oder klein?
Getrennt oder zusammen?**
7./8. Klasse
ISBN 3-580-63804-1

Aufsatz: Erörterung
9./10. Klasse
ISBN 3-580-63806-8

Protokoll und Referat
9./10. Klasse
ISBN 3-580-63807-6

**Rechtschreibung:
Groß oder klein?
Getrennt oder zusammen?**
9./10. Klasse
ISBN 3-580-63803-3

**Rechtschreibung:
Konsonanten und Vokale**
9./10. Klasse
ISBN 3-580-63802-5

Rechtschreibung: Zeichensetzung
9./10. Klasse
ISBN 3-580-63805-X

Englisch

Adjektiv, Adverb, Substantiv, Pronomen
7./8. Klasse
ISBN 3-580-63854-8

Die Zeiten – Bildung und Verwendung
7./8. Klasse
ISBN 3-580-63851-3

if-Sätze und Futurformen
7./8. Klasse
ISBN 3-580-63855-6

Die Zeiten – Bildung und Verwendung
9./10. Klasse
ISBN 3-580-63852-1

if-Sätze und Futurformen
9./10. Klasse
ISBN 3-580-63856-4

Mathe

Bruchterme und Bruchgleichungen
8. Klasse
ISBN 3-580-63901-3

Quadratische Gleichungen und Ungleichungen
9./10. Klasse
ISBN 3-580-63903-X

Je 80 Seiten, mit Lösungsteil zum Heraustrennen

Mentor — Eine Klasse besser.